SCHOOL-BASED BUDGETS

SCHOOL-BASED BUDGETS

Getting, Spending and Accounting

JERRY J. HERMAN, Ph.D.

Author and Consultant

JANICE L. HERMAN, Ph.D.

Professor and Department Head
Educational Administration
Texas A&M University at Commerce

TECHNOMIC
PUBLISHING CO., INC.
LANCASTER · BASEL

School-Based Budgets

a**TECHNOMIC** publication

Published in the Western Hemisphere by
Technomic Publishing Company, Inc.
851 New Holland Avenue, Box 3535
Lancaster, Pennsylvania 17604 U.S.A.

Distributed in the Rest of the World by
Technomic Publishing AG
Missionsstrasse 44
CH-4055 Basel, Switzerland

Printed in the United States of America
10 9 8 7 6 5 4 3 2 1

Main entry under title:
    School-Based Budgets: Getting, Spending and Accounting

A Technomic Publishing Company book
Bibliography: p. 109
Includes index p. 113

Library of Congress Catalog Card No. 96-61791
ISBN No. 1-56676-508-0

For our former colleagues in school districts and universities,
over all of the years and the miles traveled together,
who have enriched and enhanced our journey
with both the gift of their professional talents
and the pleasure of their company

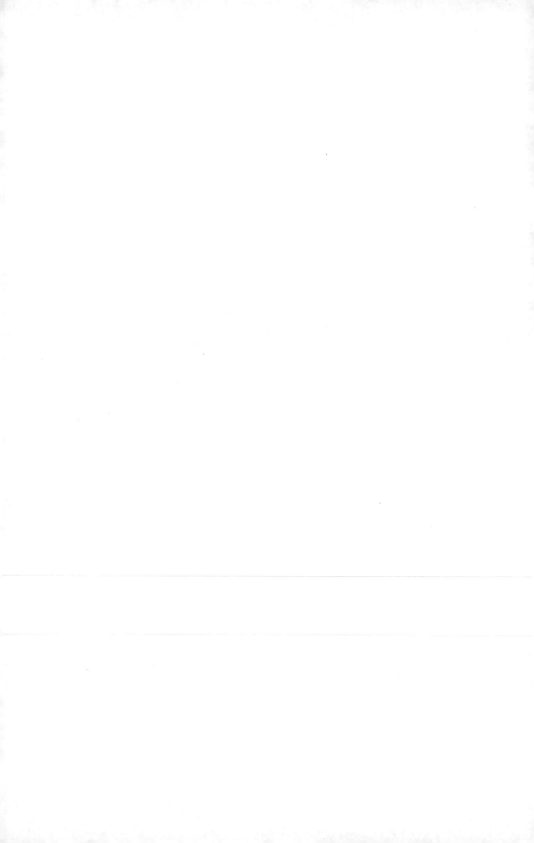

CONTENTS

WHAT THIS BOOK IS ABOUT

IN A FEW school districts across the country, school-based or site-based budgeting existed for many years before it became nationally popular. When the states of Kentucky and Texas mandated school districts and individual schools to implement school-based management (SBM) as a part of their school reform acts of 1990, the topic and the procedures became a national interest. Soon after 1990, numerous states and individual school districts became interested in implementing school-based management as a means of becoming more effective institutions and as a means of placing accountability for the quality of education at the primary delivery level—the school building site.

This movement towards SBM gained momentum from numerous sources. The major reasons for this increased movement were (1) research indicated that better decisions could be made in closer proximity to the delivery area—the school site; (2) legislatures sometimes took a statewide stand favoring SBM; (3) school board members with business backgrounds had experience in site-based movement (an example is the creation of the Saturn plant by General Motors Corporation), and put pressure on the school administrators to implement it in their school districts; (4) parents and citizens wanted more to say about decisions related to their children's schools, and SBM was a means of accomplishing this; and (5) superintendents, principals, and teachers who believed in sharing decision-making power gained approval from their boards of education and their school communities to attempt SBM.

With the advent of public interest in SBM came the task of inventing a different type of budgeting system—one that delegated many tasks of developing a budget, expending the allocated funds, and controlling those expenditures in a way that did not exceed the allocation to the site level. This book explores various ways of developing school site-based budgets, and it is written to assist the reader in understanding and developing school site budgets.

This book is written so that that after reading its information-laden four chapters, the reader will know how to build a school site budget, how to spend the available resources wisely, and how to control and account for the expenditures in a manner that keeps within the budget allocated. It is replete with examples, and a special feature is the presentation of a total central or school-based budgetary methodology. A hallmark of the book is the large number of district budgetary and accounting forms taken from actual school districts. They serve both to illustrate and provide models for adaptation by the reader.

In addition, the book will present information on the following:

- the basics of financial matters that affect school districts and individual school buildings
- the methodology, persons' roles, and rationale for site-based budgeting
- the relationship between the central and site levels
- the income, expenditure, and accounting responsibilities
- the opportunities and obligations of the principal, assistant principals, teachers, and classified employees, school site councils, and central district officials related to the total budgeting, expenditure, and control processes

FOR WHOM THIS BOOK IS WRITTEN

This book is written as an easily read, practical guide for educators and citizens who are currently involved in or who desire to become involved in school-based management and the budgetary processes involved in it. This guide should assist board of education members, principals, teachers, superintendents of schools, central and site level administrators, and citizens who serve on site-based councils to understand the concepts, processes, and value of site-based budgeting.

It will also be a valuable resource for university students studying to become principals or superintendents, and it will be an invaluable aid to university professors who teach finance courses.

BY WHOM THIS BOOK IS WRITTEN

This book is written by two authors who have had numerous years of experience with school site-based budgeting processes. One has been a superintendent of schools who utilized site-based budgeting in the districts where he served as superintendent. The other has been involved with site-based budgeting as a principal of a large school building. Together, they have also carried out a national study on school-based management, and they have written extensively on SBM and on the budgetary processes involved in implementing this contemporary management system.

JERRY J. HERMAN
JANICE L. HERMAN

## CHAPTER 1

The Basics of School Finance and School Site-Based Budgeting

THIS CHAPTER DISCUSSES: (1) the sources of school district income, (2) the sources of school building income, (3) innovative sources of additional building level resources, (4) three keys to effective budgetary planning, (5) three keys to efficient budgeting, (6) types of budgeting systems, and (7) areas of budgetary decision-making delegation. The chapter begins by emphasizing the importance of school site-based budgetary decision makers understanding the macro-district's financial situation because the school district's income, expenditures, control, and auditing structures and processes have an immediate and crucial impact upon the structure and processes utilized on the school site-based budgetary operations.

SOURCES OF SCHOOL DISTRICT INCOME

Although a school district may receive income from grants, gifts, investments, sale of property, and bond issues, practically all school districts receive the great majority of their operational income from three major sources. These sources include the federal, state, and local levels of income generation.

Types of Federal Sources of Income

There are three types of federal aid to school districts. Types of aid include categorical aid, block grants, and general aid. *Categorical aid* is granted to support a specific program, such as special education grants. *Block grants* are sums of money granted a district that cover a multitude of categories for which the money can be expended. *General federal aid* is a sum of money granted a school district for use for educational programs as determined by local authorities within established guidelines.

1

Most federal aid is designated for specified programs, the majority of which are aimed at vocational training and increasing of educational opportunities for handicapped and disadvantaged students [1].

For most school districts, the percentage of income from federal aid makes up a very small percentage of the total school district income. Also, much of the federal money is *flow-through money* given at the state level, and this money then is dispersed to the school districts based upon a federally-approved and state-operated program that determines the specific financial distribution to each school district. In addition to federal aid, practically all school districts in the nation receive a percentage of their total budgetary income from the state level. The amount of money and the percentage of a total school district's budget varies by state and by the percentage balance between locally raised district funds and state aid allocations to each district. Some states fund a high percentage of the budgets of local school districts, while others fund a very small portion of the total local district's income. It is quite common in state aid formulas to provide a higher percentage of the local school district's budgetary income in districts with a small local tax base and a lower percentage of the local school district's budgetary income to districts that have a high tax base. There are some state requirements for districts to set a minimum-effort local taxation level in order to qualify for participation in the state formula disbursement [2].

Types of State Sources of Income

Most states generate their income on the basis of property taxes, sales taxes, and income taxes. Consumption taxes are a larger category that encompasses all sales taxes levied on products and services. Excise taxes apply to specific items, such as alcoholic beverages or tobacco products. Sometimes there are value-added taxes on items such as minerals, lumber, and some manufactured items during various stages of development.

Once the state has determined the amount of money it has to operate all of its programs and meet all of its obligations, it determines the amount to be allocated to the school districts of the state. Generally, each state develops a state-aid formula for the distribution of funds to school districts. No state has a completely standard formula for the distribution of funds to the school districts because all state-aid formulas are the result of historical political actions by state legislatures over long periods of time. Most states' plans can be grouped into state aid formulas called foundation plans.

A foundation plan is generally based upon the local school district levying at least a minimum millage (a mill is .001 cents) or dollars per hundred dollars of assessed valuation in order to receive state aid. Because school districts within states vary considerably in their tax bases, most state aid formulas provide a greater amount of money to those districts that are poor in property value than they do to those districts that are rich in property value. Although it is not a totally leveling guarantee, on a continuum, the richer the property tax base of a district, the lesser the state aid; and the poorer the property tax base of a school district, the greater the state aid [3].

The third area of income, and for most school districts the major source of income, is generated at the local level. The sources of local income vary.

Types of Local Sources of Income

Most school districts in the United States receive their locally generated income from one or both of the two basic sources of ad valorem (property) taxes or sales taxes. In addition, some school districts derive local income from income taxes; and a very few school districts derive income from sumptuary (sin) taxes on items such as alcohol, tobacco, and gambling and/or severance taxes on items such as minerals when they are extracted from the earth.

Income taxes and sales taxes are largely self-descriptive. An income tax is a tax levied on the income of corporations and individuals. A sales tax is income generated when a percentage of an item's purchase price is taxed at the time of sale.

Property tax is somewhat more complex. Although personal property, such as a car, is sometimes taxed, in most cases the tax is levied on land and buildings owned by businesses and individuals. In general, a property tax is allegedly levied on a percentage of the true market value of each piece of property. The assessments are rarely totally accurate, even when some states have a state assessor equalize the local assessor's over- or underassessment of the property. In most cases, the assigned value of the property is adjusted to an agreed-upon percentage of market value when it is sold [4].

A simple example of an individual's home will illustrate how local income is generated by taxing property that lies within the geographic boundaries of the school district. Let's assume that you own a home that you bought for $100,000 a few years ago. Now that home has a market value of $150,000. The local assessor assessed the value of your home years ago at $25,000 for tax purposes, and the state assessor indicated that it was underassessed by the local board of assessment. The state assessor added a multiplier of 2.0 to determine the value for tax purposes. Thus, the home was valued at $50,000 because this state assessed property at 50 percent of its fair market value.

Once we determine that the property is valued at $50,000 for tax purposes, we only have to determine the number of mills levied against the property. Let's assume that the local school district has a voted millage rate of twenty mills. Your tax is then computed as $50,000 × .001 = $50 × 20 mills = $1,000 annual property tax. Obviously, the income received by the district would be the total accumulation of all property values times the amount of millage.

In actuality, numerous issues are associated with property tax assessment. Exemptions, tax abatements, and underassessment of property erode the tax base, but it remains the most stable economic base and provides the most dependable revenue stream.

Now that we have an overview of how income is generated at the district level, we can see what amount of this income may reach the building site level. More important, we can determine how this money is generated into the local school building site budget.

SOURCES OF SCHOOL BUILDING LEVEL INCOME

There are two major sources of income that are generated by the local school building site level. (In addition, non-income gifts of equipment, supplies, and staff development resources may free some school site monies for purposes other than those originally planned in the budget).

Income Allocated from District Level Sources

In practically all school districts that are involved in site-based management and its related school site-based budgeting process, a series of allocations are made from the district level to the building level. This money, then, can be used in a manner that the building level budgetary decision makers desire.

Although a comprehensive example, including the procedures and forms utilized by an actual school district is provided in Chapter 4, let's assume that the district level and building level budgetary decision makers agree that each school will receive $40 per pupil to be used in any legal manner the school level decision makers determine to purchase supplies and equipment or for staff development. In a school of 1,500 students, this allocation would equal $60,000 in site-based discretionary funds. Obviously, other matters, such as allocations for personnel, travel, and other operational costs, could be added if there is central district/ school building level budgetary agreement on these matters [5].

Income Generated by the School Site Level

Not all building level income has to be generated by the school district's fiscal allocation to the school building. A school building's decision makers can generate additional sums through a variety of means. They can successfully apply for grants from the state and from foundations for specified purposes, they can generate school-business partnerships that will assist with some funding needs, they can organize booster groups that will generate funds for specific purposes, and they can initiate a local school's foundation program that solicits gifts over an extended time period.

Additional Non-Income Resources Generated by the School Site Level

In addition, the local school building site can shift some of its available funds if it is able to generate non-income resources for which its budgetary funds would have to be expended [6]. The authors know of actual situations where school districts have acquired a piano for every elementary room by asking community residents to donate excellent, but rarely used, pianos that they purchased for their now-grown children. They also know of businesses that have contributed computers and software to schools. Another example occurred when a mid-sized Michigan school district was given an undeveloped eighty-acre island within the school district's boundaries to be used for an all-season nature study area for the district's students. In addition, garden clubs donated two pontoon boats to transport the students to and from the island.

INNOVATIVE SOURCES OF ADDITIONAL BUILDING LEVEL RESOURCES

The message is this—be innovative. Let your community know of the items that you wish to obtain for the students and teachers but cannot fit into your normal budget expenditures. People will respond if they know there are realistic needs that can help students by those needs being filled. Again, resources can be generated in addition to those allocated from the school district level by innovative methods such as (1) writing and obtaining grants, (2) soliciting and accepting gifts, (3) obtaining school/ business partnerships, (4) developing a local foundation program, (5) involvement in a variety of fund-raising activities, and (6) other innovative methods of increasing the resources that can be utilized to generate more comprehensive and higher quality instructional programs for the children and youth housed in the local school building [7].

Now that we have developed the income and resource possibilities available to the school building budgetary decision makers, we can explore methods of effectively planning budgets. This discussion is followed by information related to efficient budget planning.

THREE KEYS TO EFFECTIVE BUDGETARY PLANNING

There are three important functions related to effective budgetary planning. These functions are clearly indicated by the equilateral triangle illustrated in Figure 1.1.

The Educational Plan

All school building budgets should be based upon their educational programs and activities. These programs and activities should be determined after a comprehensive needs assessment has been conducted. Following this needs assessment, all programs and activities should be listed in priority order, in order to fund those programs with the highest needs priority if sufficient funds are not available (and they very seldom are) to meet all of the identified needs. Each responsible budgetary decision maker should list each program and each activity, indicating the desired level of funding required and the minimum level of funding that will allow the program or activity to exist [8,9].

Figure 1.2 presents the forms used in a large New York school district to assist site level budgetary managers to present all of their requests on a priority order and with desired and minimal levels of funding. The forms

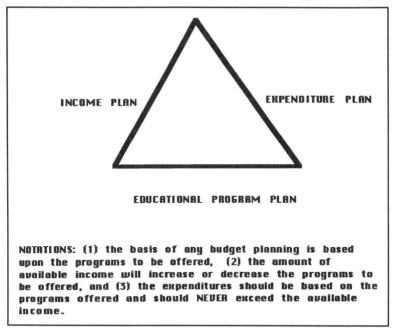

INCOME PLAN   EXPENDITURE PLAN

EDUCATIONAL PROGRAM PLAN

NOTATIONS: (1) the basis of any budget planning is based upon the programs to be offered, (2) the amount of available income will increase or decrease the programs to be offered, and (3) the expenditures should be based on the programs offered and should NEVER exceed the available income.

Figure 1.1 Local budget equilateral control triangle.

are identical except that one copy is labeled "desired level" and the other copy is labeled "minimal level." Two forms are used for each program or activity.

The Income Plan

Once all the desired programs and activities are derived from the local building's needs assessment and have been costed out, the building decision makers have to project all the anticipated income and all the non-income resources that interface with the desired programs and activities. This projected income must match the programs and activities that are to be offered eventually. If the income is less than all the desired programs and activities, the lowest priority needs must be eliminated or modified in order to meet the available income.

It is crucial that the local building budgetary decision makers project well into the future. A comprehensive needs assessment is crucial, and in cases where the district allocates funds to the local school building budget decision makers on a per pupil basis, it is equally important to make a

			Estimated cost			
Rank	Program/ Activity	Support/ Justification	Salary	Supplies	Equipment	Total

Location/Budget Manager

Figure 1.2 Large New York State school district's site-based budget planning document.

sophisticated projection of the number of pupils anticipated in future years [10]. For example, if a school building now services 1,000 pupils and receives $40 per pupil in the current year, it will have a total of $40,000 to expend. However, if it is predicted that in the subsequent year, the school building will house only 900 pupils, it is clear that only $36,000 will be available from the district level to run all the desired programs and activities. Having this advance knowledge, the local school building budgetary planners can attempt to find other sources of income to make up the predicted financial deficit, or they can plan cuts in those programs and activities that will least adversely affect the students.

The Expenditure Plan

Once the programs and activities have been decided upon, based on the priority order established by the comprehensive needs assessment and the actual available income, the expenditure plan can be placed into operation. Controls must be established to ensure that the expenditures do not exceed the available income and that the expenditures are directly related to the high-priority programs and activities that have previously been agreed upon.

The key to effective budgetary planning is to make all areas, educational plan, income plan, and expenditure plan, equal to one another. If programs exceed income, programs have to be cut. Conversely, if income exceeds programs, enriched programs can be offered. If expenditures exceed income, major consequences will affect the school building site budgetary managers. If one thinks of the three axes of an equilateral triangle, all axes must be kept equal at all times [11].

Now that we have explored effective budget planning, let's consider the keys to efficient budgeting. They are income-generation sources, expenditure controls, and accounting procedures.

THREE KEYS TO EFFICIENT BUDGETING

Income-Generation Sources

Income generation requires an entrepreneur's spirit, coupled with the standard sources of income that are allocated to the building level by the school district central operation. Grants from various governmental and private sources are possible, gifts from individuals and corporations are possible, fund-raising by various school building level groups are possible, and non-income resources that free up the budgetary monies for other purposes are possible. The combination of all these sources will assist the school building educators in offering the most comprehensive, high-quality, cost-effective programs and activities that are possible within the total income generated.

Expenditure Controls

Once the income has been confirmed and the programs and activities put into operation, it is crucial that controls on expenditures are initiated. Some of the most important controls include: (1) a fiscal management information system (MIS) [12]; (2) accounting procedures that reflect standard classifications for revenues, expenditures, and balance sheet items; (3) dual activity income collection and deposit; (4) prompt bill payment in order to collect the discounts offered for rapid payment, and

(5) establishment of an accountability structure entitled zero-sum budgeting.

Fiscal Management Information System

A fiscal MIS is simple to establish but crucial to efficient and effective budgetary operation. Each program and budget control responsibility is coded for computer retrieval. This can be done by the district business office and accessed by modem from the school building site. If the district does not have this computer network established, the local school building person(s) responsible for expenditures and budgetary control can establish her/his (their) building level MIS by assigning appropriate retrieval codes to each program and budgetary responsibility location within the school building [13]. Once the codes are established, all that is necessary is the retrieval of information under three categories.

For example, (1) a series of codes is established, (2) a column is established for the initial budgeted amount, (3) a column is established for year-to-date expenditures under each coded item, (4) a column is established for encumbered funds, and (5) a column is established for unencumbered/available funds [14]. This procedure will allow those responsible to continuously monitor expenditures to determine if they are operating within the allocated dollar amount. If it appears that, at any point in the year, that any account is overexpending to date, adjustments can be made prior to running into a deficit condition. The format for this MIS will simply look like that shown in Figure 1.3.

Accounting

Accuracy and accountability while obtaining income and the expenditure of funds is critical. A *general* (control) ledger is established that has two columns: a *debit column* under which income is registered as received with the date and amount noted and a *credit column* under which

Program Item Code	Budget	Expenditures to Date	Encumbered Funds	Unencumbered/ Available Funds
A-100-06 B-200-07 Others				

Figure 1.3 *School-based fiscal MIS structure.*

each expenditure is recorded by the amount expended and the date the sum was expended. The second part of a double-entry system is a series of *subledgers* by specific programs and items of expenditures. As an expenditure is made, a credit is registered in the general ledger and a debit is made in the appropriate subledger. For example, if supplies in the amount of $26 were purchased for a first grade reading program, $26 would be taken out (credited) in the general ledger, and $26 be registered (debited) as an expenditure in the appropriate subledger established for supplies for the first grade reading program. This procedure also assists in monitoring, at any time, the total budgetary unencumbered income in the general ledger, and it also allows the monitoring of the total sum expended per date for each subledger account that has been established [15].

Dual Activity Income Collection, Accounting, and Deposit

In order to avoid mistakes or theft, it is important to put into operation a dual activity income collection and deposit structure. Since school buildings often collect fees from athletic programs and other programs offered by the school, and since many clubs and booster groups operate in conjunction with the school, it is important to establish controls. First, the principal should have an official list of those persons who are authorized to collect, account for, and deposit money; and second, if there is to be a significant amount of income generated, it is wise to have key individuals bonded. Also, whenever tickets are sold, the tickets should be numbered, and the number of tickets sold at a stated price should be exactly reconciled with the amount of money deposited in the bank.

Once the persons responsible are clearly identified, one person should be responsible for collecting the money while a second person should be responsible for double-counting the money received and depositing the same in a bank. For night activities, it is important that the deposit bag(s) is acquired from the bank and that the income from the night activity is immediately counted, bagged, and deposited in the bank's night depository by the responsible party [16].

Paying Bills to Collect Discounts

Whether the local school building officials are authorized to pay for purchases directly, or, as is true in most cases, the school district's business office pays the bills accrued by all school buildings, it is important to take every discount offered [17]. Many suppliers offer as much as a 15 percent discount if the bill is paid within thirty days and up to a 10 percent discount if the bill is paid within sixty days. The suppliers offer this because it gives them ready funds to invest or operate. *Cash flow* is important to the suppliers because it permits them to operate without borrowing funds and paying interest on them.

For the school building budgetary decision makers, taking advantage of discounts is also very important. Each dollar saved by speedy payment of amounts owed provides additional money to be allocated to support and/or enhance the educational programs and activities offered the students.

Zero-Sum Budgeting System

A zero-sum budgeting system makes each person who has budgetary responsibilities within the school building responsible for living within the budgetary allocation provided while allowing flexibility, as needs may change throughout the year. The system is simple and very effective. Each responsible party may wish to change the items to be purchased from those items that were initially to be purchased by some or all of the allocated funds. All that the responsible party has to do is to replace those items that were to be purchased in a manner that frees up a like amount of money for the revised purchases [18]. In some cases, this exchange may require additional approval by the building principal, depending on the accountability structures operating within the individual school building.

This system allows flexibility as needs change throughout the year, and it keeps the total expenditures 100 percent in line with the budget allocated. Moreover, it makes each budgetary functionary totally accountable for wise purchases and for living within her/his budget allocations.

Accounting and Auditing Procedures

The final phase of the total budget process involves accounting and auditing procedures. An example of a school building site accounting system of book ledgers was provided earlier. However, the importance of audits must also be stressed. An audit is an investigation of the appropriate and legal expenditures of funds. It is wise to appoint someone in the building as internal auditor, or the district might have an official internal auditor who will audit the school building level accounting procedures and books [19]. In any case, practically every school district will employ an external auditor to conduct an audit and write a report to the superintendent and the board of education each year.

The external auditor or auditing team will also investigate the budgetary procedures, controls, and expenditures at the building level [20]. At the building level, auditors are especially interested in the method of bookkeeping and accounting and in the specific ways that internal activity (sports events, musical events, clubs, and booster activities) funds are handled. Some basic control decisions should be instituted as operating principles for use by those responsible for activity funds. They include the following:

- Maintain two completely separate and independent sets of records of receipts and expenditures.
- Keep the persons who have the authority to expend monies distinct and separate from the person(s) who are the custodians of those funds.
- Initiate procedures that will ensure a rapid and careful examination and check upon each receipt and each payment.
- Make certain that at least two individuals take part in each act of disbursing monies.
- Initiate audits, at least on an annual basis [21,22].

An audit is basically conducted on a sampling basis, but if something looks suspicious, great detailed investigations are undertaken by the auditor. The auditor's report will complement the district on things that it is doing well, and the report will also recommend procedures to strengthen the budgetary operations of the district and the school building. It is an important process, and each principal should welcome this assistance.

Now that we have completed our discussion of the three keys to efficient budgeting operations, let's turn to an investigation of the types of budgetary systems. It will become clear that any or a combination of all these systems can be utilized within a school site-based budgeting structure.

TYPES OF BUDGETARY SYSTEMS

There are five basic types of budgetary systems. Clearly, each type has its own strengths and weaknesses, but when assembled into a comprehensive fiscal management information system (FMIS), they unite to become a very strong and important tool for use by those who plan, control, and operate the budgets of the district and the individual school buildings.

Function/Object Budgeting

Function/object budgeting is a system that enters anticipated, and later actual, expenditures in the budget ledgers under a coded basic *function*, such as administration or instruction. The system also enters expenditures under coded *objects*, such as salaries, supplies and materials, equipment, and other expenditure categories. This function/object budget system is used in many school districts, and it is still the required format for many reports issued to other governmental agencies [23].

Function/object budgeting is historically the most commonly used system across the school districts in the United States, and it remained the most popular system until the advent of software budgetary programming popularization of the Program Planning Budgeting System (PPBS) format that gained national attention when U.S. Secretary of Defense Robert McNamara initiated it as a means of controlling wasteful practices in the military budgets. The weakness of function/object budgeting is that it is too general in nature; and it does not provide sufficient information to evaluate individual programs offered by the schools. A brief coded hypothetical example is provided in Figure 1.4 [24–26].

Program, Planning, Budgeting, Evaluating, System (PPBES)

Program budgeting can easily be explained by stressing what is meant by each of the subparts of the title. *Planning* involves the generation of

```
01 (general fund budget code)
01-11100-00-100 Administration (function)    Total  $_____
01-11100-00-100-01 Salaries (object)                $_____
01-11100-00-100-02 Supplies (object)                $_____
01-11100-00-100-03 Equipment (object)               $_____

01-11100-00-200 Instruction (function)       Total  $_____
01-11100-00-200-01 Salaries (object)                $_____
01-11100-00-200-02 Supplies (object)                $_____
01-11100-00-200-03 Equipment (object)               $_____
```

Figure 1.4 *A coded example of function/object budgeting.*

goals and specific objectives; *programming* involves the generation of alternative activities and services designed to achieve the specific objectives; *budgeting* provides the dollars attached to each *program* activity and service designed to achieve each objective (also the stage where plans are formalized and money is accounted for) and reporting structures are devised; *evaluating* involves the collection, arraying, and analysis of data in a manner that allows decisions to be made as to whether or not the objectives were achieved within the fiscal resources allocated to them; and *system* refers to the fact that when all four of the aforementioned parts are intricately linked together, a continuous system exists [27].

Many federally funded programs require use of what is commonly known as *program* budgets. Also, some school districts utilize program budgeting for various locally funded programs. In any case, it is suggested that the school site budget be prepared and administered from a program budget format to provide the maximum amount of control, to involve many individuals in budget responsibility and accountability, and to provide the maximum amount of output information to assist in the making of wise future educational and budgetary decisions. A brief example of PPBES is shown in Figure 1.5.

The strength of PPBES for the local school building site persons who are responsible for the budget is that it is a powerful tool for directly relating each expenditure to the achievement of a specific program goal and its objectives for each program funded. It allows the principal and others involved in the budget process to conduct a cost/benefit analysis at any period in time.

Zero-Based Budgeting

Zero-based budgeting (ZBB) reached its height of popularity when Jimmy Carter was governor of Georgia. ZBB is a system that requires every person who is charged with budget building to defend every expenditure requested on the basis of a projected cost/benefit. This involves providing alternative activity suggestions for each expenditure level and arriving at a final determination of the expenditure level included in the budget [30]. That is, if three funding levels are projected, the decision makers will determine which of the three levels provides the biggest results for the amount of money to be expended. It is a cost/benefit analysis that is designed to achieve the biggest results "bang" for each dollar expended.

STEP ONE: PLANNING

General Goal: To improve second grade reading in Typical Elementary School.

Objective: To increase the reading scores in Typical Elementary School from 40 percent of the students scoring above the national norm to a minimum of 60 percent scoring above the national norm in a matter of a two-year period.

STEP TWO: PROGRAMMING

Cooperative Learning Will Be Initiated. Cooperative learning involves a system of instructional delivery that places a group of students of differing abilities in an environment that allows working together as a cooperative team to enhance each student's learning. It is based upon the belief that sometimes students can learn some things better from working with other students, rather than from only working with a teacher. Of course, the teacher still structures, oversees, and monitors the students' activities.

A Large Number of Retired Persons Will Be Recruited to Serve as Volunteer Tutors for Individual Children Who Are Having Difficulty with Their Reading. Again, the teacher will control what the volunteers do and how they interact with the student or students assigned each volunteer. This system is designed to provide more guided assistance to each student and to provide a positive supportive and motivational environment in which students will learn.

STEP THREE: BUDGETING

At this step, all account codes are assigned and the dollars allocated to each program. All expenditures, such as salaries, supplies and materials, equipment, fringe benefits, training, and other expenditure categories related to that program are accounted for under the specific accounting codes assigned each program. Thus, a very accurate accounting of expenditures allows identification of a total cost per specific program and, if desired, for each student to be determined. This, then, can allow a cost/benefit analysis to be made related to the outcomes (results) achieved by the designed instructional delivery systems [28].

STEP FOUR: EVALUATING

During this stage, all the expenditure and student achievement data are arrayed and analyzed, and an evaluation is made to determine whether or not the specific program objectives have been met, within the time frame agreed upon and within the dollar amounts allocated to that specific program.

STEP FIVE: SYSTEM

This step is the completion of the PPBES structure. It is the point at which all subelements are integrated into an articulated and smoothly operational budgetary continuous systems approach [29].

Figure 1.5 Example of program budgeting procedures.

ZBB usually includes the essential parts of identifying (1) a *decision unit* that is usually the lowest level at which budget decisions can be made [31]. For example, it could be the English department in a specific high school within the school district; (2) a *decision package* that includes a goal statement and specific objectives, an evaluation structure, and a minimum of three funding levels [32]. Together, these elements concisely describe the budget implications for each decision unit. In each of the three expenditure scenarios, the cost of each expenditure item (salaries, benefits, supplies and materials, capital outlay and other categories of expenditures) is outlined; (3) a *ranking* of each decision package to be considered [33]. This involves the ranking of every decision package and projecting the costs and benefits anticipated for each of the three funding levels suggested for each decision package and from every decision unit source; (4) *agreement and allocation of funds* includes the decisions related to which packages and at which level within each package are to be included in the final approved budget; and (5) *budget preparation* involves assigning account codes to each budgetary expenditure item, within each decision package, and relating these to each decision unit of responsibility. Once the budget is approved, all expenditures are accounted for within the systems that are designed to accommodate ZBB.

The major strength of ZBB is that it causes each person who has budgetary unit responsibility to submit decision packages for each program or activity that she/he wishes to undertake within the unit for which the person is responsible. In addition, each person holding budget planning and expenditure control responsibilities must provide three levels of funding for each desired program or activity, and this procedure is done on a cost/benefit basis. That is, the ratio of benefits must be equal to or greater than the costs associated with achieving those benefits before a budgetary allocation is made. The concerns related to ZBB and PPBES in their purest forms are (1) a great deal of training must take place before implementing ZBB, and (2) it requires a tremendous amount of every budget manager's time to build an entirely new budget based upon the desired programs and activities for each subsequent year [34].

School-Based Budgeting

School or site-based budgeting (SBB) is a system that allows a specific school building site to make budgetary decisions that have traditionally been reserved for the central school district office area. Decisions related to staffing, instructional programs, supplies and materials, equipment, and many other decision areas that affect budgetary expenditures have to be negotiated between the central school district's budgetary decision makers and the school site budgetary managers prior to implementing SBB [35]. Many times this process involves only the principal, but it also can involve school building employees and a school-based management council comprised of representative employees, parents, community residents, and the principal [36]. An example of SBB in operation is provided next.

The central decision makers agree that a school building site will receive a certain allocated number of teachers, secretaries, food service workers, clerks, aides, and custodians; the site will also receive a specific budgetary amount for expenditures related to the various categories of employee salaries and their related fringe benefits. Within these parameters, the site manager(s) (and, perhaps, the site-based management council) can decide on the persons to be hired and the expenditures of the allocated funds for personnel purposes.

In addition, the site-based budgetary manager(s) may be given a specific dollar amount to be expended for such matters as (1) supplies and materials, (2) capital outlay, (3) consultant services, and (4) employee training. Within the budgetary expenditure parameters established, the site-based fiscal decision makers can expend the funds in any manner that they feel best fits their identified needs. A *need* is defined as a gap or discrepancy between what is and what should or could be. Of course, each of these areas to be negotiated can result in (1) some being relegated totally to the site level, (2) some decisions being reserved for the district level, and (3) some decisions being shared between the school building site level and the central school district level.

The major strengths of SBB are (1) it allocates decision-making power to the level closest to the operation—the delivery of instruction to the students, and (2) it involves a variety of people. When this method is combined with school-based management councils, stakeholders should have the delegated power to make decisions related to the educational and support programs offered the children and youth to be educated at the school building site level.

One concern related to SBB is that much prior training has to take place before moving from a traditional centralized fiscal decision-making operation to a site-based decision-making operation. This is especially true if school-based management councils are to be involved in budget-related decisions. In addition, unless centralized, agreed-upon parameters, controls, and evaluation systems are in place, the district could have multiple school building site units, for all practical purposes, operating within one legally constituted school district. Some of these individualized school building site operations might improve under SBB and others might deteriorate and offer a lesser quality educational program than that previously presented under the centralized system. In such cases, waste and inefficiency may result [37].

Advantages of an Integrated Fiscal Management Information System of Budgeting

Any or all of the three (function/object, PPBES, and ZBB) systems can work within the structure of school site-based budgeting [38]. This became possible with the advent of high-powered computers that can store a tremendous amount of data and which allow multiple account codes to be utilized for various budgetary systems and purposes.

In order to take advantage of the strengths of each of these systems, an integrated budgeting system that includes some modifications of a purist's methodology is suggested for use at the school site-based budget level. This structure will

- utilize site-based budgeting (SBB) with the support of a representative site-based council
- use traditional function/object budgeting account codes to allow production of official reports that require this budgeting structure
- depend on PPBES as an accounting code structure tied to individual programs as an outcome analysis system that allows decision makers to decide what costs are associated with any level of program or activity detail that they desire. This allows the budgetary decision makers to perform a cost/benefit analysis for each situation. By analyzing the results and discovering the outliers (those situations where the cost/benefit ratio is extremely favorable and those where the cost benefit ratio is extremely unfavorable), program elements that appear to be extremely favorable can be introduced into other venues [39]. On the other hand, an improvement team can be established to develop plans to eliminate the existing elements that are causing the negatives within the very poor cost/benefit delivery venue.

- utilize ZBB with every new program or activity introduced for a three-year period. Also, modify the system in a manner that causes each person responsible for a budgeting unit to provide an alternative budget for each existing program that is suspect that includes a (1) 5 percent budgetary increase, (2) 0 percent increase, (3) 5 percent decrease, and (4) 10 percent decrease for the subsequent budget year [40].

With the advent of microprocessors and advanced software programs, and with the desire to move many fiscal decisions to the operational school building site level, there is ample reason to combine function/object, PPBE, ZBB, and SBB into a single powerful systems approach to budget building, control, and accountability. No school system should settle for one budgetary approach when a combination of all budget systems can be utilized to develop a FMIS that will allow a thorough evaluation, on a cost/benefit basis, of the programs and activities offered the students at each school building [41].

Once the expenditures are arrayed and a cost/benefit or other type of evaluation is conducted, the budgetary decision makers can make wise educational decisions. These decisions can then be incorporated into a recycling phase designed to improve the subsequent year's budget building and expenditure controls. The ultimate purpose is to provide students with the highest quality educational programs and activities possible within the approved budgetary money allocations.

Now let's turn to an operating procedure that is designed to control budgetary expenditures during the fiscal year within which the budget is made operational. Zero-sum budgeting (ZSB) is a powerful control system that is advised for use at the school building site level.

Zero-Sum Budgeting

ZSB is an operational structure that makes all persons responsible for budget matters at the school building site level accountable for expenditure decisions and for keeping those decisions within the amount of money allocated, while allowing flexibility of expenditure decisions throughout the fiscal year. If the individual budget manager wishes to change the previously planned item(s) of expenditure to another item(s) of expenditure, all that is necessary is to get agreement with the building principal to do this and to provide budgetary adjustments that will reduce, in exact dollar amounts, the previously planned expenditures that now can be expended on the newly agreed-upon expenditure(s).

A FINAL WORD

It is important that those individuals responsible for establishing, operating, controlling expenditures, and auditing for accountability of school site-based budgets understand the basics of school finance, the necessary interface between district and school site levels of budgeting, and the school site-based structures and processes that are required to operate effectively and efficiently. Obviously, this knowledge will require some information sharing and training for those who are to operate, for the initial time, with school site-based budgeting. Only when all this knowledge is effectively and efficiently put into practice can individuals and groups responsible for school site-based budgets perform their budgetary functions well.

REFERENCES

1. Swanson, A. D. and R. A. King. 1991. *School Finance: Its Economics and Politics.* White Plains, NY: Longman, pp. 195–220.
2. Burrup, P. E., V. Brimley, Jr., and R. R. Garfield. 1993. *Financing Education in a Climate of Change.* 5th ed. Boston: Allyn & Bacon, pp. 336–338.
3. Jones, T. H. 1985. Introduction to *School Finance: Technique and Social Policy.* New York: Macmillan, pp. 105–112.
4. Odden, A. R. and L. O. Picus. 1992. *School Finance: A Policy Perspective.* New York: McGraw-Hill, pp. 102–105.
5. Herman, Jerry J. 1992. "School-based Management: Sharing the Resource Decisions." *NASSP Bulletin,* 76 (545): 102–105.
6. Lane, J. J. 1986. *Marketing Techniques for School Districts.* Reston, VA: Association of School Business Officials International, pp. 101–121.
7. Epstein, J. L. 1995. "School/Family/Community Partnerships: Caring for the Children We Share." *Phi Delta Kappan,* 76 (9): 701–712.
8. Odden, A. R. and L. O. Picus. 1992. *School Finance: A Policy Perspective.* New York: McGraw-Hill, p. 271.
9. Wagner, I. D. and S. M. Sniderman. 1984. *Budgeting School Dollars: A Guide to Spending and Saving.* Washington, DC: National Association of School Boards, pp. 1–22.
10. Herman, J. J. 1988. "Map the Trip to Your District's Future." *The School Administrator,* 45 (9): pp. 16, 18, 23.
11. Drake, T. L. and W. H. Roe. 1994. *School Business Management: Supporting Instructional Effectiveness.* Boston: Allyn & Bacon, pp. 69–79.
12. Herman, J. L., J. J. Herman, and T. Raymer. 1994. "Improving Budget Decision Making: Incorporating a Fiscal MIS (Management Information System)." Paper presented at the Association of School Business Official's Annual Convention, Seattle, October.

13. Burrup, P. E., V. Brimley, Jr., and R. R. Garfield. 1993. *Financing Education in a Climate of Change.* 5th ed. Boston: Allyn & Bacon, p. 393.

14. Burrup, P. E., V. Brimley, Jr., and R. R. Garfield. 1993. *Financing Education,* p. 392.

15. Rebore, W. T. and R. W. Rebore. 1993. *Introduction to Financial and Business Administration in Public Education.* Boston: Allyn & Bacon, pp. 145–150.

16. Drake, T. L. and W. H. Roe. *School Business Management,* p. 72.

17. *Ibid.,* p. 91.

18. Herman, J. L., J. J. Herman, and T. Raymer. 1994. "Improving Budget Decision Making."

19. Burrup, P. E., V. Brimley, Jr., and R. R. Garfield. 1993. *Financing Education,* p. 396.

20. Drake, T. L. and W. H. Roe. *School Business Management,* pp. 114–116.

21. Burrup, P. E., V. Brimley, Jr., and R. R. Garfield. 1993. *Financing Education,* p. 351.

22. *Ibid.,* p. 346.

23. Odden, A. R. and L. O. Picus. 1992. *School Finance,* p. 258.

24. Rebore, W. T. and R. W. Rebore. 1993. *Introduction to Financial and Business Administration,* p. 108.

25. Burrup, P. E., V. Brimley, Jr., and R. R. Garfield. 1993. *Financing Education,* p. 377.

26. *Ibid.,* p. 386.

27. Drake, T. L. and W. H. Roe. *School Business Management,* p. 77.

28. Kaufman, R. and J. Herman. 1991. *Strategic Planning in Education: Rethinking, Restructuring, Revitalizing.* Lancaster, PA: Technomic Publishing Co., Inc., pp. 116–123.

29. Burrup, P. E., V. Brimley, Jr., and R. R. Garfield. 1993. *Financing Education,* p. 378.

30. Bliss, S. W. 1978. *Zero-Base Budgeting.* Reston, VA: Association of School Business Officials International, p. 30.

31. Pyhrr, P. A. 1973. *Zero-Base Budgeting: A Practical Management Tool for Evaluating Expenses.* New York: John Wiley & Sons, p. 62.

32. *Ibid.,* p. 78.

33. Bliss, S.W. 1978. *Zero-Base Budgeting,* pp. 33–40.

34. Odden, A. R. and L. O. Picus. 1992. *School Finance,* pp. 298–299.

35. *Ibid.,* p. 305.

36. Herman, J. J. and J. L. 1993. *School-Based Management: Current Thinking and Practice,* Springfield, IL: Charles C Thomas, pp. 106–108.

37. Herman, J. L., J. J. Herman, and T. Raymer. 1994. "Improving Budget Decision Making."

38. Rebore, W. T. and R. W. Rebore. 1993. *Introduction to Financial and Business Administration,* p. 108.

39. *Ibid.*

40. Drake, T. L. and W. H. Roe. *School Business Management,* p. 72.

School-Based Budgeting: Players and Resources

CHAPTER 2 PRESENTS information related to the following areas: (1) identifying the different persons responsible for site-based budgetary decision making and the roles each person plays in that process, (2) conducting needs assessment as a means of developing budget income and expenditure priorities, (3) specifying the relationship between the central school district and local school building site levels related to the budget planning, expending, controlling, and auditing functions, and (4) determining areas of budgetary delegation to be decided upon that will allow the school building site level persons responsible for school level budgets to make important budgetary decision within a format and policies that have been agreed to by the central office and school site levels. The chapter ends with a final word and a series of exercises.

Each school district must develop its own pattern of delegated responsibility for budgetary decisions—as it truly is a locally designed matter. We begin the discussion by identifying the budget's players and determining their specific budgetary roles.

THE PLAYERS AND THEIR SITE-LEVEL BUDGETARY ROLES

Building Principal

The local school building principal is a key player in any scheme that incorporates local school site-based budgeting. Site-based budgeting merely allows someone or some group to make budgetary decisions related to building level needs, rather than making those decisions at the traditional, central school district level [1]. Therefore, site-based budgeting could be done by merely allowing an autocratic building principal to make local budget decisions, without involving any other person or group of people in the process.

In theory and in practice, however, the principal will include many others in the processes of budgeting, expending, controlling, and accounting. The numbers and categories of persons involved will vary with the structures and processes approved by the central school district level and by the willingness of the building principal to share the important decisions related to the local school budget. Numerous possibilities for involvement of a wide variety of categories of persons exist.

No matter, however, what exact budgetary decision making structure and processes are put in place, the principal is still the single most important local school player. She/he: (1) can make decisions in an autocratic manner, (2) can involve teachers and other employees, or (3) can work with a school-based management council consisting of parents, teachers, community members, classified employees, or any combination of these [2].

Other Building Level Administrators and Supervisors

Some of the other administrators, especially in a large high school, might well include the following persons who have budgetary responsibilities: (1) assistant principals, (2) music director, (3) athletic director, (4) director of counseling services, (5) subject area and/or grade level department chairs, (6) food service director, and (7) director of custodial and maintenance services.

Assistant Principals

Assistant principals can be involved in planning, spending, and controlling local budgetary funds in a variety of ways. In a large school, they can be considered the budget managers for a series of departments, or they can each be made the budget manager for a grade level. In addition, an assistant principal could be made the budget manager for athletics and all cocurricular activities.

They could be assigned budgetary managerial responsibilities related to instruction, personnel, purchasing, or other specific planning and control functional areas. In any case, their budgetary input is important to the teachers and other employees, as well as to the principal of the building.

Building Level Music Director

In schools with a comprehensive music program that includes vocal groups, orchestra groups, instrumental groups, and marching bands—all of whom have subgroups and all of whom participate in multiple performances, it is the wise principal who appoints a director of music as the budgetary manager to work with the music staff. The purchasing of musical instruments, the cost of transportation, the purchasing of uniforms, added to many other expenditures, can add to a considerable sum of money. A wise principal will work with this manager to ensure that these needs are met and will rely on this manager to monitor and control expenditures within the income allocated to the music programs.

Building Level Athletic Director

In a large school, a full-time athletic director may be hired. If an athletic director is not in place, it is crucial that an assistant principal or some other person is named as the one responsible for the planning, expending, controlling, and accounting for budgetary matters. Let's take a quick look at a comprehensive high school athletic program's offerings to see the substantial costs involved, even if some income is derived from those athletic events that are popular with community members.

A large high school's comprehensive athletic program might well include any, or all, of the following: (1) football, (2) hockey, (3) basketball, (4) track, (5) cross country, (6) wrestling, (7) volleyball, (8) gymnastics, (9) swimming, (10) field hockey, (11) soccer, (12) tennis, (13) baseball, (14) softball, and (15) lacrosse. Costs related to these athletic programs include such matters as transportation, coaches salaries, officials, uniforms, ticket takers, police, ambulance, doctors, and other expenses for meals and lodgings for athletes and coaches.

Again, a wise principal will solicit all the help she/he can in this area from those who have the greatest amount of knowledge. The principal is advised to name a single individual as budget manager for the area of athletics [3].

Building Level Subject Area and/or Grade Level Department Chairs

At the small elementary school level, the principal may wish to work directly with all employees and a school-based council on budgetary matters. The principal of a small elementary school may also want to relegate the needs assessment process and the budgetary matters to a lead teacher at each grade level who will become the budget manager [4].

Building Level Food Service Director, Director of Custodial and Maintenance Services, and Other Classified Personnel

If these functions are not controlled by the central office level, then the principal should involve the central office staff in determining the needs for their area and make these persons responsible for purchases within the budgetary allocation. Even if these functions are controlled at the central district level, they should be made to feel a part of the operating team within the building [5].

Teachers and Other Certified Personnel

Teachers and other certified personnel should be given an integral, important part in all aspects of budgetary matters. They are the individuals closest to the student clients, they are the individuals who will deliver the instructional programs, and they are the individuals who will establish the classroom climates within which the students will learn [6]. Therefore, having the most detailed knowledge and having to deliver the products and services to the student client qualifies them to conduct a needs assessment and effectively utilize the items to be purchased.

Classified Personnel

Classified personnel such as secretaries, clerks, and teacher aides must have a say in the equipment and supplies that are necessary to do their support roles efficiently and effectively. For example, a clerk who does not have an adequate computer or software, but who is expected to keep massive and accurate records, cannot perform the expected support duties. Therefore, it is important that the principal and other budget managers assist classified personnel in their needs assessment, for these individuals are important, and they can make or break a positive climate [7].

Central Office Administrators

In addition to the local building personnel that should or could be involved in the budgeting process, other central administrators might be helpful in the planning stages of budgeting. For instance, the assistant superintendent for instruction may provide knowledge about newly available curriculum materials or teaching supplies, or the central office media director may have advance knowledge of new instructional computer software that might be helpful to the teaching staff [8].

Assistant Superintendent for Financial Matters

No matter who else may or may not be involved in the budgetary process related to local school site budgeting, one individual will always be involved in site-based budgeting. The assistant superintendent for finance will work directly with the building principals in the process of allocating funds, purchasing or expending funds, controlling expenditures, and accounting. These matters are usually done on a one-to-one basis between the school building principal and the assistant superintendent (or business manager) for finance.

The assistant superintendent for finance distributes the district's planning forms, controls the budget-planning calendar dates, provides weekly or biweekly budget account balances reports, and often takes care of the noninstructional purchases related to the school building level for food services, transportation, custodial, and maintenance services. It is crucial that the working relationships between building principals and this district level functionary are interactive, positive, and productive [9].

Superintendent of Schools

The superintendent of schools performs the important tasks of (1) getting the board of education to approve school site-based budgeting, (2) obtaining the cooperation of all central functionaries in this process, and (3) defending the decisions made at the building level to the board of education and to the general public [10].

The superintendent who is involved in school site-based management districts served as the initiator, the innovator, the cheerleader, and the defender of site-based budgeting. She/he is the person who has the most contact with the greatest number of persons in the district, and she/he must be a believer in school site-based budgeting.

Board of Education

The board of education as a whole, and the individual members of the board, are also important players in the implementations and continuance of local school site-based budgeting. It is they who: (1) must give formal approval to move from the traditional budgeting system to a site-based process, (2) must convince the community members that this is a wise move, and (3) must defend the process. Summarily, the board members must also be cheerleaders for and defenders of the process of site-based budgeting [11].

School-Based Management Councils

School-based (site-based) management has become a very popular new structure added to the school districts all across the nation in the last ten or so years. It came into being by legislative mandate in 1990 in the states of Kentucky and Texas; it has been initiated by board of education mandates or by the granting of board permission; and it has been introduced by innovative superintendents of schools, principals, teachers and teacher unions [12]. In most places where school-based decision making has been initiated, it has been done for the purposes of (1) making better decisions at the level where the processes and products take place and (2) involving employees and community members in decisions that affect the education of the children of the individual school building. In any district where school-based management exists, some form of site-based budgeting usually exists [13,14].

Kentucky Education Reform Act of 1990

One has only to review the power provided to school-based management councils by the legislature of Kentucky when it ratified the Kentucky Education Reform Act of 1990 [15]. The details related to site-based management included the following, and it is easy to determine the impact these decisions would have on the local school's site-based budget.

1. By January 1, 1991, the school board shall adopt a policy for implementing the school-based decision-making approach, and policies related to KRS 160.340 must be amended to further implement this approach related to professional development activities (sections 2 and 3 of HB 940).

2. Each participating school shall form a school council composed of two parents, three teachers and the principal or administrator. More can be added, but the proportion must remain the same. Parents cannot be related to any school employee.

- Teachers shall be "elected" for one-year terms by a majority of teachers.
- Parents shall be "selected" by the members of the PTO of the school; or, if none exists, by the largest organization of parents formed for this purpose.
- The principal or head teacher shall chair the council.

The councils' and principals' responsibilities include:

(1) Set school policy to provide an environment to enhance students' achievement and meet the goals of sections 2 and 3 of this act. The principal shall be the primary administrator and instructional leader of the school; and, with the assistance of the total school staff, shall administer the policies established by the school council and school board.

(2) All staff "may" be participants. The staff shall divide into committees according to their areas of interest. A majority of each committee's members shall "elect" a chair to serve a one-year term. Each committee shall submit its recommendations to the school council for consideration.

(3) The council and each committee shall determine the agenda and frequency of meetings. The meetings shall be open to the public with the exceptions provided in KRS 61.810.

(4) Within the funds available from the school board, the council shall determine the number of persons to be employed in each job classification at the school, and can make personnel decisions on vacancies. It cannot recommend transfer or dismissals.

(5) The council shall determine which instructional materials and student support services shall be provided in the school.

(6) From a list of applicants recommended by the superintendent, the principal shall select personnel to fill vacancies, after consultation with the school council.

(7) To fill a principal vacancy, the school council shall select from

among those persons recommended by the superintendent, and the superintendent shall provide additional applicants upon request.

(8) The council shall adopt a policy to be implemented by the principal in these additional areas:

- determination of curriculum, including needs assessment, curriculum development, alignment with state standards, technology utilization, and program appraisal within the local school board's policy
- assignment of "all" instructional and noninstructional staff time
- assignment of students to classes and programs
- determining the schedule of the school day and week subject to the beginning and ending times and school calendar set by the school board
- determining the use of school space during the school day
- planning and resolving issues regarding instructional practices
- selecting and implementing discipline and classroom management techniques; including the roles of students, parents, teachers, counselors, and principals
- selecting extracurricular programs and determination of policies relating to student participation based on academic and attendance requirements, program evaluation, and supervision

3. The local board policy on school-based decision making shall also address:

- school budget and administration (discretionary funds; activity and other school funds; funds for maintenance, supplies and equipment; and accounting and auditing)
- assessment of individual student progress, including testing and reporting of student progress to students, parents, the school district, the community, and the state
- school improvement plans, including the form and function of strategic planning and its relationship to district planning
- professional development plans developed pursuant to sections 12 and 13 of this act
- parent, citizen and community participation including the relationship of the council with other groups
- cooperation and collaboration within the district and with other districts, public agencies and private agencies
- requirements for waiver of district policies

- requirements for record keeping by the school council
- a process for appealing a decision made by a school council
- in addition, the school board "may" grant to the school council any other authority permitted by law

4. The school board "shall" make liability insurance available to all members of the school council when performing duties as school council members.

5. After the effective date of this act, any school in which two-thirds (2/3) of the faculty vote to implement school-based decision making may do so.

6. By June 30, 1991, each school board shall submit to the chief state school officer the name of at least one (1) school which has decided to implement school-based management. If no school so votes, the school board "shall" designate one (1) school to implement it.

All schools shall implement school-based management by July 1, 1996. However, by a majority vote of the faculty, a school performing above its threshold level requirement, as determined by the Department of Education, may apply to the State Board for exemption from this requirement.

7. The department of education shall develop sample guidelines to assist local boards in the development of their policies, and it shall provide professional development activities to assist schools in implementing school-based decision making.

8. A school that chooses to have a different school-based model than the one outlined, can request an exemption by describing the model, submitting it through the board of education to the chief state school officer and the state board for approval.

It is clear that the Kentucky legislature did not intend to conduct the school district business of the state on a business-as-usual basis. It mandated that much power be delegated to the school building site level and that nontraditional, site-based, decision makers be involved in those decisions important to education at the local school building level. It is also clear that these new players were to be involved in many important budgetary matters. Kentucky is a dramatic example, but many other school districts across this nation have opted for school-based management and made the commitment to site-based budgeting.

Now that the case for site-based budgeting has been clearly established, we turn to the beginning of any good budgeting process. Conducting needs assessments is the initial step to be taken, and this process is discussed next.

CONDUCTING NEEDS ASSESSMENTS

The initial step in any budget planning is the conduct of a needs assessment. A *need* is defined as a gap or discrepancy between what is and what should or could be. A needs assessment should not be a request by everyone for a wish list [16]. Indeed, it is best done in a very logical and comprehensive manner. Since this should be the initial step in budget planning, the values of conducting a needs assessment and details of the process follow.

The values of a needs assessment are many. The main values are: (1) It involves all school building functionaries, (2) it assesses what is, (3) it determines what should or could be, (4) it allows the prioritizing of needs, (5) it is proactive planning, (6) it focuses on gaps or discrepancies that exist, (7) it causes action plans to be developed to meet the identified needs, and (8) it focuses on end products/results over specified time periods [17].

A needs assessment can be conducted by collecting data on what exists in the current state of the school's affairs. A pair of examples will clarify this concept.

(1) In general, elementary students at Typical School are scoring below average on norm-referenced testing, and they are also doing poorly when measured by criterion-referenced testing. When the students at Typical School, who possess relatively the same demographics and school history as the students in Exemplary School, are compared to the Exemplary School's students, they fall far short in achievement in language arts, mathematics, and science. This identifies a very important need that is of the highest priority to be addressed.

(2) At Typical High School, where the student body is multiracial, a great frequency of conflict exists between and among all races. This conflict is also a very important need to be addressed. The faculty and administration of Typical High School implement a program of student mediation in an effort to reduce the number and severity of conflicts.

In both cases, many budget implications exist. For underachievement: (1) Are more teachers or aides required? (2) Are different supplies, equipment, and teaching materials required? and (3) Do training programs have to be established for teachers, aides, and administrators?

To reduce conflicts between and among the students at Typical High School, many budget implications also exist: (1) Do trained mediators have to be hired to work with the students? (2) Do teachers, administrators, and others who work with the students require training? and (3) Should students and teachers visit other schools where student-mediation programs have been successfully implemented [18]?

Data to be collected when conducting a needs assessment include both hard (factual) data and soft (attitudinal or opinion) data. Both types are important to collect, analyze, prioritize, conduct action programs on, and evaluate the results of the action programs implemented. Some examples of hard and soft data to be collected at the individual school building level follow.

Hard Data

- student achievement levels in all subject areas. Test data will be disaggregated by student category, and test data will also be item analyzed.
- student dropout rates
- student absenteeism and tardiness rates
- teacher turnover rates
- graduate follow-up data in terms of success in further educational institutions and on the job [19]

Soft Data

- school climate
- student attitudes
- employee attitudes
- parents' attitudes
- community attitudes

Now that we have dealt with the values of conducting a needs assessment and provided a few examples of data to be collected, we turn to the steps in the process [20]. There are seven steps to be followed:

(1) The participants agree to plan using data from a needs assessment.
(2) They identify the actual needs assessment method to be utilized and the planning partners to be involved.

(3) They obtain participation from the identified planning partners.

(4) They collect agreed-upon hard and soft data.

(5) They list the identified, documented, and agreed-upon needs.

(6) They prioritize all needs in terms of their importance to resolve existing problems and then reconcile the priority disagreements among the planning partners.

(7) They finalize the list of needs to be resolved and work out action programs to cause the desired resolution to occur.

Now that our needs assessment has been completed, we can address the monetary requirements to be included in the budget. First, however, we must decide which areas will be the responsibility delegated to the local school building site level, which will be retained by the central school district administrative level, and which will be shared between these two levels of budgetary decision makers [21].

BUDGETARY RELATIONSHIP BETWEEN CENTRAL DISTRICT AND BUILDING SITE LEVELS

Budget Planning

Budget planning can take place in three ways. First, the local school building site can be given a set dollar amount for various categories, such as equipment and supplies, and within this dollar amount (and within certain statutory guidelines), those responsible for the budget at the local school building level can make any decisions that they desire. Second, the central school district administrative level can make all budget decisions and simply inform the local school building principal of those decisions. Third, there can be cooperative planning between those responsible for budgetary matters at the local school building site level and the central school district administrative level.

In most cases, the budgetary decision making will be totally done at the central school district administrative level, or it will be a shared planning process between the individual school building level and the central administrative level. The specifics will have to be negotiated and decided upon for each school district [22].

Budget Expenditures

Once it is decided to allocate funds to the local school building site level, this task can be accomplished in two major ways. First, a lump sum amount can be allocated to the local school building, and this sum can be expended in any manner that the local budgetary manager(s) decide. Second, budgetary allocations can be given for specific expenditure reasons, such as staff development, travel, equipment or supplies; or budgetary allocations can be given for each specific program operated at the local school building. Finally, although not frequently utilized, a combination of allocations can be made with some being of a lump-sum nature and others being of a specific earmarked nature [23].

In general, regardless of the levels at which budget planning took place, the expenditures authorized at the school building site level are left totally to the discretion of those responsible for budgetary expenditures at that level. This arrangement allows the expenditures to be closely aligned with the identified needs at the local school building level.

Budget Accounting

With the advent of microprocessors and specialized school budget software, it is possible for the local school building to have its own budgetary account tracking code system. With a local area network permitting a local school building budget manager to log on to the school district's computer network, immediate access is provided to the budgetary status of each school building's individual accounts [24]. However, many local school building's budget managers must still rely on budgetary status reports that are provided to the school building principal every two weeks or once a month.

Regardless of the type of accounting system described above, a standardized format is utilized to report the status of the budget accounts. An example of a typical accounting report format is presented in Figure 2.1.

Budget Auditing

Auditing is customarily controlled by the central school district business office. Many districts conduct two types of auditing. An internal school district auditor periodically audits all accounts, including those related to each local school building. Also, an external auditor hired by

Name of School Building		Date of Status Report		
Account Number	Budgeted Amount	Expenditure to Date	Encumbered	Available Balance
# Supplies	$46,580	$31,235	$3,201	$12,144
# Contract Services	$16,200	$8,140	$00	$8,060
# Other?				

Figure 2.1 Budget accounts status report form.

the board of education conducts a yearly audit of all the school districts and local school building accounts [25].

An auditor will usually take a sample of each account to determine (1) if the expenditures are made in accordance with standard budget procedures and to check on fiscal statutory compliance, (2) if there are sufficient controls on income and expenditures—such as two different persons handling and depositing income funds, and if there is a double-entry accounting system. If an account looks suspicious of theft or inadequate safeguards or inaccurate records, the auditor will go into every detail to investigate the suspicious account(s). At the individual school building level, most times concerns are registered by the auditor over the operation of activity funds.

When the audit is completed, the auditor(s) provide a written and oral report to the board of education, and they also usually provide a letter of recommendation to the superintendent. The letter to the superintendent lists suggestions for strengthening the budgetary procedures for the future.

Now that we have explored the various stages of budgeting, we turn to which budgetary areas have to be decided upon between the central district and local school building site levels.

BUDGETARY DECISIONS TO BE MADE RELATED TO DELEGATION TO THE BUILDING SITE LEVEL

The key to an effective and efficient budget operation system is to predetermine, in the case of school site-based budgeting, which budgetary and budget-related decisions should rest at each level. In reality three different methodologies can be negotiated and agreed upon. They are (1) fully school site-based decision making, (2) fully central district office-based decision making, and (3) shared budgetary decision making between the school site and central school district levels [26]. Not only does one of these three areas have to be agreed upon but also the parties must be in agreement on each of the functional subareas. Figure 2.2 indicates all the areas to be explored, negotiated, and agreed upon.

Decisions Related to Instruction

In any school site-based budgeting procedure, the basic decisions related to instruction should be primarily delegated to the school site level. The only reasonable exceptions should be areas in which the board of education has mandated such programs as technological literacy educa-

DIRECTIONS: Place a check mark in each column where agreement has been reached on the budget related matters to be delegated to the appropriate decision model.		
Shared Area of Decisions	District Level	Building Level
1. Staffing and Hiring	_____	_____
2. Curriculum	_____	_____
3. Instructional Method	_____	_____
4. Equipment	_____	_____
5. Supplies and Materials	_____	_____
6. Transportation	_____	_____
7. Food Services	_____	_____
8. Custodial Services	_____	_____
9. Maintenance Services	_____	_____
10. Athletic Programs	_____	_____
11. Co-curricular Clubs	_____	_____
12. Instrumental Programs	_____	_____
13. Strings Programs	_____	_____
14. Substitute Teachers	_____	_____
15. Teacher Aides	_____	_____
16. Clerical Aides	_____	_____
17. Staff Development	_____	_____
18. Other Possible Areas	_____	_____

Figure 2.2 *Areas of school site-based decision making related to budgetary matters to be decided upon.*

tion. Many districts have a history of intensive involvement of site personnel in curriculum development and revision, in instructional projects, and in selection of methods and materials, particularly textbooks. Instruction is also an area that is heavily impacted by state department control through mandated courses of study and curricular and instructional regulation. Federal influence in this area, particularly in categorical fund programs, is considerable, and it is possibly, then, a site-based decision-making implementation area of more perceived sensitivity and critical nature than hiring or budget making [27].

The ultimate concern about curriculum and instruction responsibility being lodged at each site level is the need to ensure, within district guidelines, a minimum quality program and a reasonable distribution of higher cost and more administratively complex programs, such as special education. If each school exercises curricular and instructional entrepreneurship, then very distinctively different programs may emerge at each school; each one's fidelity to the common district core of academic goals and objectives must be demonstrated to the parents and community, and, possibly, for accreditation purposes, to other governing bodies and agencies.

Decisions Related to Personnel

This is an area where compromise might be preferred to that of all decisions related to the hiring and placement of employees. It seems reasonable that the central level will advertise openings, locate candidates, and complete any official paperwork (especially regarding compliance with affirmative action and equal employment opportunity regulations) that is required. A reasonable compromise might be for the local school people, including the school-based management committee, to interview and recommend the candidate of the local decision makers' choice [28]. Again, the cooperative procedure might apply to all categories of employees, but it could also be limited to teaching employees.

Involvement in hiring and assignment of employees is a key empowerment factor of site-based decision making and one of the most controversial. It can be viewed from a financial perspective, as a process of the allotment of teacher or employee equivalents per building and the subsequent expenditure of those equivalents by the school site decision-making team. It can also be viewed realistically as the expenditure of only additional personnel units, as they are accrued, through a collaborative interview and hiring process. Some uniformity of personnel quality should be maintained so that schools do not neglect low-profile personnel services, such as media specialists and librarians and to prevent any temptation to increase discretionary funds by understaffing or hiring inexperienced or part-time employees. Districts experienced in site-based budgeting allow schools to hire teachers on an average-cost basis, with the site paying a flat, predetermined rate for each teacher, regardless of the teacher's actual salary.

Decisions Related to Budget Planning and Expenditures

Although any of the three methodologies could be utilized, it would appear that the wisest decision making can best be made at the local building level for those matters most directly affecting the local school's programs, students, parents, and employees and that the central office decision makers retain total control of those items that most directly affect the central school district's operation. Some areas, such as custodial or maintenance services might best be decided in a shared manner [29].

Some decisions regarding the operation of schools can be made centrally; those that require a degree of uniformity for purposes of efficiency, economy, or understanding. Examples include uniform wage scales and employee benefits, resource entitlements, accounting and reporting, matters of public welfare, and relationships to other governmental agencies. Consideration should be given to the centralized efficiencies of volume purchasing and of warehousing versus allowing all purchases of commodities such as duplication paper or maintenance supplies to be purchased on an individual consumer basis by each school.

Once the basic methodology has been decided upon and the areas of delegation have been agreed to, the local school building site budget managers should have complete discretion on the expenditure of the funds allotted to that school site. Only in this way will those closest to the students have the most to say about the wisdom of each expenditure.

Decisions Related to Other Central and Site Level Matters

In each school district there are other specific matters that may have to be decided upon. For example, in many school districts where school site-based management exists, any school building's functionaries can petition the board of education to make exceptions or waivers to policies or standard operating procedures for just cause. When granted, these exceptions may also have budgetary implications. Additionally, site budgeting demands accounting preparation that may need to be sufficiently pliable to be transformed into any statutory format or auditing purposes. A school district may need to maintain two sets of financial accounts—one that is state mandated and one that is locally designed to facilitate site budgetary use [30]. The critical review of expenditure patterns is redirected from the central administrative unit to the school building administrative unit. The central office requires a continuous flow of current information concerning local building level operations. Data processing capability is a prerequisite for developing workable decentralized budgeting processes. The only financial decisions to be justifiably retained at the central administrative office are those

- that do not directly affect the teaching-learning process
- with an inherent capability of producing efficient, large-scale financial economies
- that have systemwide application as a result of imposed statutes or contractual agreements
- with overall cutbacks imposed by budget cutting review agencies

In dealing with public monies, there is always a requirement for openness, accountability, prudence, adequate planning, independent auditing, and good fiscal stewardship. To meet these conditions, the decentralization process needs a planned structure. Measures of comparability can only be applied to data assembled in standard formats. Within the confines of a budgetary recording and reporting system, there must be provision for capitalizing on adaptability to local needs. This can be accomplished by a process that accommodates structured transfer of funds or a realignment of allocated funds.

Safeguards would ensure that such financial shifts be well planned, visibly executed, and decided upon using such logical bases as shifting enrollments, changes in program emphases, staff replacements, new technology or method, or unforseeable circumstances.

A FINAL WORD

In order for schools to be the best they can be for students, it seems reasonable that decisions affecting those students be made by the persons who are closest to the delivery of instruction to those students. In all cases this will, at a minimum, involve teachers and building principals, but this may also involve school-based management councils composed of parents, school community members, as well as school building employees.

Because the traditional standard control structure has neither produced the student achievement levels desired nor involved the community in decisions related to its students, a call has gone out for more involvement of nontraditional decision makers and for more important decisions to be delegated to the local school building site level. School site-based budgeting must accompany this new decision-making model. Only as financial resources are made accessible to the local school building site level can the decisions made in the interest of the local school building's students be made operational and accomplished.

EXERCISES

(1) Write job description areas related to budgetary matters for each of the budget functionaries you think should be included in the budget process at the local school building site level and at the central school district administrative level.
(2) Decide how you would go about conducting a comprehensive needs assessment. Include the hard and soft data you would collect, the planning partners you would include, and the process steps you would utilize.
(3) Give ten examples each of hard data and of soft data that you would collect for your school's needs assessment.
(4) Which areas do you feel should have decision making totally delegated to the local school building site level, which areas totally kept at the central school district administrative level, and which areas shared between the local school building site level and the central school district administrative level?

REFERENCES

1. Peel, H. A. 1994. "What It Takes to Be an Empowering Principal." *Principal,* 73 (4): 41–42.
2. Kirby, P. C. 1994. "Principals Who Empower Teachers." *Journal of School Leadership,* 4 (1): 39–51.

3. Herman, J. J. and J. L. Herman. 1994. *Educational Quality Management: Catalyst for Integrated Change.* Lancaster, PA: Technomic Publishing Company, Inc. pp. 81–83.

4. Herman, J. J., J. L. Herman, and V. Oliver. 1995. "A Study of School-Based Management in Selected Southern States", *International Journal of School Reform,* 4 (4): 60–66.

5. Ford, D. J. 1992. "Chicago Principals under School Based Management." Paper presented at the Annual Meeting of the American Educational Research Association, San Francisco, April.

6. Herman, J. J. and J. L. Herman. 1993. *School-Based Management: Current Thinking and Practice,* Springfield, IL: Charles C. Thomas, Publisher, pp. 44–59.

7. Herman, J. J. and J. L. Herman. 1994. *Making Change Happen: Practical Planning for School Leaders.* Newbury Park, CA: Corwin Press, pp. 97–99.

8. Herman, J. J. and J. L. Herman. 1993. *School-Based Management,* pp. 97–109.

9. Herman, J. J. and J. L. Herman. 1991. "Business Officials and School-Based Management." *School Business Affairs,* 57 (11): 34–37.

10. Herman, J. J. 1991 "School-Based Management: An Introduction." *School-Based Management: Theory and Practice.* Reston, VA: National Association of Secondary Principals, pp. v–vii.

11. Knarr, T. C. 1992. "A Matter of Trust." *American School Board Journal,* 178 (11): 44–45.

12. Herman, J. L. and J. J. Herman. 1993. "A State-by-State Snapshot of School-Based Management Practices," *International Journal of Educational Reform,* 2 (3): 89–94.

13. Oswald, L. J. 1995. *School-Based Management: Rationale and Implementation Guidelines.* Eugene, OR: Oregon School Study Council.

14. Herman, J. J. and J. L. Herman. 1992. "Educational Administration: School-Based Management," *The Clearing House,* 65 (5): 261–263.

15. Herman, J. J. and J. L. Herman 1993. *School-Based Management: Current Thinking and Practice,* Springfield, IL: Charles C. Thomas, pp. 191–194.

16. Kaufman, R., J. J. Herman, and K. Watters. 1996. *Educational Planning: Strategic, Tactical, Operational.* Lancaster, PA: Technomic Publishing Co., Inc., pp. 100–102.

17. Herman, J. J. 1990. "Action Plans to Make Your Vision a Reality," *NASSP Bulletin,* 74 (523): 14–17.

18. Herman, J. J. and J. L. Herman. 1997. *Individual and Group Problem Solving Techniques in Schools.* Lancaster, PA: Technomic Publishing Company, Inc.

19. Herman, J. J. and J. L. Herman. 1994. *Educational Quality Management: Catalyst for Integrated Change.* Technomic Publishing Company, Inc., pp. 41–42.

20. Herman, J. J. and J. L. Herman. 1991. *The Positive Development of Human Resources and School District Organizations.* Lancaster, PA: Technomic Publishing Company, Inc., pp. 126–128.

21. Herman, J. J. 1992. "School-Based Management: Staffing and Budget Expenditures." *School Business Affairs,* 58 (12), pp. 24–25.

22. Shortt, T. L. 1994. "Teachers Can Become a Vital Component of the School Budget Process." *NASSP Bulletin,* 78 (566): 39–46.

23. Odden, E. R. and P. Wohlstetter. 1995. "Making School-Based Management Work." *Educational Leadership,* 52 (5): 32–36.

24. Herman, J. J. 1990. "School-Based Management: A Checklist of Things to Consider." *NASSP Bulletin,* 74 (527): 67–71.

25. Burrup, P. E., V. Brimley, Jr., and R. R. Garfield. 1993. *Financing Education in a Climate of Change.* 5th ed. Boston: Allyn & Bacon, pp. 347–348.

26. Odden, A. R. and L. O. Picus. 1992. *School Finance: A Policy Perspective.* New York: McGraw-Hill, pp. 302–304.

27. Holman, L. J. 1995. "Should Site-Based Committees Be Involved in the Campus Staffing Process?" *NASSP Bulletin,* 79 (569): 65–69.

28. Fossey, R. 1992. "Site-Based Management in a Collective Bargaining Environment: Can We Mix Oil and Water?" Paper presented at the Education Law Seminar of the National Organization on Legal Problems of Education, Breckenridge, CO, February-March.

29. Conley, S. C. 1993. "A Coalitional View of Site-Based Management: Implications for Administrators in Collective Bargaining Environments." *Planning and Changing,* 22 (3–4): 147–159.

30. Herman, J. J. and J. L. 1993. *School-Based Management: Current Thinking and Practice,* Springfield, IL: Charles C. Thomas, pp. 186–190.

School-Based Budgeting: Major Issues and Examples

CHAPTER 3 PRESENTS numerous examples of methodologies and forms utilized by a variety of actual school districts. It presents discussions related to the areas of: (1) budget planning, (2) budget expenditures, (3) budgetary controls, (4) budget accounting, and (5) budget audits. Numerous sample forms are provided, and the chapter ends with a final word and some exercises.

BUDGET PLANNING

All budget planning should be based upon a comprehensive needs assessment; a projection of the number of anticipated students; a projection of the number of the various categories of employees required to effectively and efficiently serve the students; a projection of expenditures for equipment, supplies, materials, and services; and a budget calendar. Examples of methodologies for each of these categories will clarify the various areas required to plan an effective and efficient budgetary structure and process. The preplanning required before a budget is officially adopted and initiated is the key to successful budgeting.

Developing a Budget Calendar

In every school district and in every school building, budget managers have, in reality, a two-year period for which they are actively dealing with budgetary matters [1]. For the current budget year, budget managers are receiving funds and authorizing expenditure of these funds within the money available. In addition, the budget managers are planning for the subsequent school year, and sometimes they are projecting budgets for as many as five years into the future.

Advance planning is crucial to excellent budget development and management and can be done best when numerous persons are involved in the budget processes by establishing a budget calendar. An effective budget calendar will indicate the date at which different tasks and activities must take place, and it will list the individuals responsible for performing each task [2].

An example of a budget calendar from an actual small Tennessee school district is provided in Figure 3.1. Note that this is a fiscally dependent district that must obtain approval of the city council. Many districts are fiscally independent and do not have to obtain approval of another agency. Also, an early (K–2) elementary school building principal, within this school district, provides the following input requests to her teachers.

Date	Budget Preparation Process
12/11/95	1. Board of education considers adoption of 1996–1997 budget preparation calendar.
1/1/97 to 3/1/96	2. Principals, teachers and support staff prepare budget requests. Department supervisors and support staff prepare budget requests.
3/4/96	3. Principals submit budget requests for schools. Department supervisors submit budget requests for departments.
3/5/96 to 5/6/96	4. Superintendent and the board of education's budget committee review budget requests and receive public input on the development of a tentative budget.
5/13/96 to 5/22/96	5. Superintendent submits a tentative budget to the board of education.
	6. Board of education considers the superintendent's tentative budget.
	7. Board of education adopts a tentative budget and advertises it for public input.
	8. Superintendent presents tentative budget to employees. NOTE: After the board of education has adopted a tentative budget, it must advertise it in the newspaper for at least two weeks (14 days) before it can be considered for final adoption. Therefore, the board of education must adopt a tentative budget on or before Thursday, May 2, 1996, in order to consider adopting a final budget at the regular monthly board of education meeting on June 10, 1996.
6/10/96	9. Board of education considers changes to the 1996–1997 tentative budget.
	10. Board of education adopts the 1996–1997 school year budget.
6/17/96	11. Superintendent and board of education chairperson present the 1996–97 school budget to the city's mayor and city's council.
7/1/96	12. Beginning of the 1996–1997 fiscal year.

Figure 3.1 *Example 1996 budget planning calendar for a small Tennessee school district.*

TEACHER INPUT BUDGET—CLASSROOM ALLOTMENT FOR 1996–1997

- I would like feedback on the amount of increase (if any) that is needed for your 1996–1997 classroom allotment.
- Consider the amount of money you are allotted for your classroom for the 1995–1996 school year and make a recommendation for 1996–1997.
- This should be discussed at K–2 grade level and a report turned in by grade level. Support personnel may turn in individual requests.
- Consider that more than a 10 percent increase would be above average.
- Justify your requests.
- Please report this recommendation to me on the form provided.
- Discuss this at the grade level meeting on January 31 and have the report to me by Friday, February 2.
- If you have no request for an increase, check no request and turn in the form.
- This form is for classroom allotment and school purchase recommendations only. Furniture requests will be made in the spring, and they will be forwarded to the business manager at that time.

The simple form used by this principal appears in Figure 3.2.

Projecting the Number of Students

Along with conducting a comprehensive needs assessment, projecting the numbers of students to be served in the subsequent school year is crucial to projecting budgetary income requirements; it is also crucial in the allocation of budget expenditures. The most common method for projecting future numbers of pupils is called the "cohort survival" method of pupil projection [3]. It is important that a student projection be completed for every school building site in the school district, as well as the district as a whole. This method is provided in Chapter 4 in Figure 4.3.

Projecting the Number of Categorical Employees Required

Once the numbers of students to attend the individual school building

Grade Level: _____ Kdgn. _____ First _____ Second
Date: _____
Classroom allotment for 1995–1996 per teacher $ _____
Classroom allotment request for 1996–1997 per teacher $ _____
NO REQUEST for additional allotment   _____
Brief description of reason for request:

_____

_____

_____

_____

_____

Purchase recommendation for:
1. Grade Level:

_____

2. School Level:

_____

Figure 3.2 Teachers' budget request form.

site are determined, it is important to match the numbers of students with the exact programs they will attend. Once this is completed, the numbers of teachers, instructional aides, coaches, and other extracurricular activity sponsors can be determined.

At the classroom level, the numbers of teachers and instructional aides are often determined by state requirements, local district policy, or negotiated union/management master contract provisions [4,5]. For example, a state may mandate a smaller number of pupils in the lower elementary grades, a local district board may mandate full-time kindergarten with no more than fifteen students in each class section, or a union/management contract may have a negotiated article that mandates an instructional aide for every two teachers.

Projecting Expenditures for Equipment, Supplies, Material, and Services

Projecting expenditures for equipment involves the estimate of the equipment to be replaced because of damage, the additional equipment required to equip any new programs to be initiated, the addition of equipment for additional students or employees, and the addition of equipment to replace outdated equipment. A good example of replacing outdated equipment is that required to maintain a state-of-the-art technology program.

Projecting expenditures for supplies and materials also involves an estimate of the number of students and employees, the specific program needs, any changes in methods of instructional delivery that are planned, and the replacement of damaged or outdated supplies and materials [6]. An example is an elementary school that decides to initiate a whole-language approach to delivering its language arts program.

Projecting the required expenditures for service involves the identification of external persons to be hired to perform staff development programs, external persons hired to supervise activities at extracurricular events, or any other situation where it is deemed appropriate to hire external persons to staff required or desired services. Examples include the hiring of a doctor and an ambulance service to be present at every football game played by each secondary school in the district.

Some school districts allocate a block grant for all purposes to be determined by the individual school building site's budget manager(s). Other school districts allocate funds for specific purposes.

A small school district's allocation for specific purposes will illustrate this structure. In addition, the school building site's decision makers may acquire additional funds by sales, fund-raising activities, grants, and gifts. An example of the structure for a school district level budget allocation to its constituent school building sites is presented in Figure 3.3.

Conducting a Needs Assessment

Conducting a needs assessment should be the first activity to take

Function	Elementary	Middle	High
11—Instruction	$25.75	$30.75	$35.75
22—Resources and Media (per school)	$386.75	$1,411.00	$4,910.00
23—Administration	$3.80	$4.00	$5.80
31—Guidance and Counseling	$3.50	$4.75	$6.90
62—Services	$1.00	$2.50	$5.75
63—Supplies	$6.00	$7.00	$8.50

Figure 3.3 *A small school district's school building site's budget allocation process (per pupil allocations).*

Step One: The local school building site conducts a comprehensive needs assessment.

Step Two: Immediate and long-range priorities are established for the classroom, grade levels, departments, programs, and school as a whole. Priorities are determined on the basis of (1) available resources, (2) norm-referenced test results, (3) criterion-referenced test results, (4) the state's basic competency test results, and (5) available funds compared to the expenditures of the previous year. *It is imperative to budget all available funds into those instructional areas where needs have been identified.*

Step Three: Determine the school building's income sources: (1) balance on hand; (2) fees; (3) state funds allocated to the building; (4) federal program funds; (5) grants received; (6) teacher fund-raising; (7) organizational fund-raising: booster groups, band, choral, athletic; and (8) income from school's athletic and other ticketed events.

Step Four: Designated funds must be expended in approved areas, and these categories of funds *cannot* be transferred into other accounts. Examples are Title One and other federal funds, grants provided for specific programs, earmarked state funds and some local funds allotted for athletics, band, and other specific activities.

Step Five: Develop teacher, grade-level, and/or department budgets. The principal is free to develop her/his local school budget site form to obtain this information.

Step Six: Develop budgets for the support areas of athletics, bands, guidance, library/media, operations, and administration.

Step Seven: Determine capital outlay needs.

Step Eight: Determine maintenance and renovation needs.

Step Nine: Compile teacher-level, grade-level, department, and administration budgets. Use Form 722-C to submit income and Form 722-B to submit expenditures.

Step Ten: After final budget figures are determined, the principal must submit her/his budget to the school district's central business office.

Figure 3.4 *School building site-based budget process.*

place when planning for future budgets. A need is the gap or discrepancy between what is in existence and what could or should be [7]. It should be conducted by involving all employees and other persons who have a stake in the quality of education taking place within the local school building in (1) assessing the quality and quantity of what is, (2) determining what could or should be, (3) analyzing the gaps between what is and what could or should be, (4) prioritizing the identified needs in order to first address those considered most important, and (5) devising action programs to eliminate the existing gaps and overcome the identified needs.

A large county school district in Alabama stresses that a needs assessment be completed as the first step in its school building site-based budget system, and this district's process illustrates the importance of conducting a needs assessment. In order to illustrate the primary point of planning in this district's site-based budgetary process, this district's ten-step budget procedure is listed in Figure 3.4.

The amount of money to be expended is illustrated by an elementary school within this large district. The elementary school serves a student population in excess of 1,000 pupils.

Total Income = $410,627.04
Total Expenditures = $410,627.04
Total Operational Income = $17,598.60
Total Operational Expenditures = $17, 598.60

Source of Income		Amount
A. State		
1. Allocation in lieu of fees	Subtotal:	$4,100.00
B. County board of education		
1. Instructional allotment per student		$358.00
2. Library		$1,074.00
3. Janitorial		$626.50
4. Vocational		00
5. Federal funds		00
6. Community schools (in kind)		00
7. Band		00
8. Postage		$161.10
9. Telephone (estimate $42.00 per month $\times$ 12)		$504.00
10. Salaries		$395,028.44
11. Other		00
	Subtotal:	$395,752.04
C. Sources of Local Funds		
1. Donations		
a. Instructional—academic		00
b. PTA		$4,000.00
2. Sales		
a. Pictures		$2,000.00
b. Supplies for students and teachers		$700.00
c. Other sales (itemize) jackets		$500.00
(1) Empathy		$75.00
(2) Field trips		$3,500.00
3. Community school		00
4. Extracurricular activities/clubs		00
5. Library		00
6. Guidance		00
	Subtotal:	$10,775.00
	A,B, & C Income Grand Total:	$410,627.04

Figure 3.5 *Breakdown of an elementary school's budget income.*

The breakdown of expenditures for this elementary school is presented in Figure 3.5.

Let's now turn to criteria that should be utilized to determine how best to use the funds available to the school building site. If we think of a school building site as a cost center, the following criteria, expressed in an interrogative format, can then be applied to budgetary decisions [8].

- How does the amount to be expended for one category of expenditures compare to the same amount being expended for other categories (cost/benefit analysis)?
- Are the limits on the amount of funds allocated to a category of expenditures beyond that amount where additional expenditure of funds will not improve the educational or program results or will not significantly improve the results when related to the degree of expenditure (cost effectiveness)?
- Are there certain categories of expenditures in which increasing the amount expended will, in all probability, increase the results of the educational offerings or program results equal to or in excess of the increased amount of expenditures (targeted allocations)?
- What budgetary actions can be taken to increase economies in all categories of expenditures (for example, purchase by economy of scale)?

BUDGET EXPENDITURES

Once the preplanning has taken place, the budget has been officially adopted, and the school building site budget established, the actual expenditure of funds can begin. For a variety of reasons throughout the year, the expenditures from the various accounts may have to be adjusted because the actual expenditures required do not always equal projected expenditures.

BUDGET ACCOUNTING AND BUDGET CONTROLS

Controlling the budget is crucial. Unlike the United States federal government, a local school building or school district cannot legally overexpend its available funds. Sometimes when drastic changes are required during a budget year, due to a reduction in state aid or an unfavorable vote on a renewable millage, numerous fiscal and human problems have to be addressed and resolved quickly.

Other budgetary controls include frequent reports of the status of budget accounts and identification of specific persons who have control of expenditures, money collection, and fund deposit functions. Internal auditing is also important. At the school level, it is crucial to have secure controls on all student activity accounts, as these are the areas in which external auditors historically cite the most problems [9].

Also, the financial records of the school district and the individual school building sites should meet the following criteria:

- For every budget account, all appropriations, appropriation transfers, expenditures, encumbrances, and unencumbered balances should be accurately recorded on a daily basis.
- For every purchase order, the name of the vendor, description of the item to be purchased, the number of items to be purchased, the dollar amount of the purchase, the name of the person authorized to let a purchase order, the date of the purchase, and the school building to which the purchase is to be delivered must all be noted. The purchase order sets must be prenumbered, and there must be an accounting for each set.

  If the amount of the purchase is of such a magnitude as to legally, or by policy, require bids, an abstract of the bids received must be maintained. The normal, and sometimes legal requirement, procedure is to award the bid to the lowest bidder unless proof exists that the bidder is in violation of the specifications upon which the bid was let or the reputation of the bidder is proven to be poor [10].
- For each purchase, besides the purchase order information above, the record of receipt, the condition of the goods received, the invoice, and the record of payment must be maintained.
- For each income account, the budget allocation, the receipts to date, and the unencumbered balance should be noted.

Budget accounting is simply a labeling methodology that assists in the accuracy and legality of expenditures. *Auditing* is the yearly terminal procedure that involves trained auditors in investigating the accounts of the central district level and the school building site level to ensure that all budgeting and accounting procedures are accurate and that expenditures have been legally made [11].

Below are a series of controls and example forms from a very large school district in Georgia. This district's budget accounting manual, with instructions for the individual school buildings, is more than 150 pages.

This district's transactions are all recorded on computers. The software permits the productions of twelve different financial reports. Each school building site can determine its financial position daily.

Accounting controls are incorporated into the daily reparation and recording or posting of financial activities, and they provide assurance that all transactions at the local school site level have been properly recorded and that all of the accounting records are in balance [12]. The major accounting controls include

- Numerical control over master receipts and local school site checks.
- Numerical control of each entry recorded through the automatic budget entry numbering system.
- Description of each receipt and disbursement that has been made and the account code to which each was credited or charged.
- Automatic recording of totals for cash receipts, disbursements, and transfers resulting in instant recording and retrieval of daily cash balances, monthly, or any time frame within the fiscal year [13] when requested by the school building site's budget manager(s). The daily cash balance will always equal the sum of the cash balances for each activity account.

BUDGET AUDITS

School districts employ an external auditor or auditing firm to conduct an external budget audit, at least on an annual basis. However, districts that wish to keep more constant monitoring of accounting procedures and accuracy and legality of financial transactions, employ an internal auditor to work full-time within the school district. Both types of auditors not only audit the school district's central books, but also audit the financial records of the individual school building sites.

The external auditor will conduct the following activities, including those related to the individual school building sites. Obviously, the internal auditor will perform similar tasks, but she/he will do so on a continuous basis throughout each completed fiscal year.

- Examine the balance sheet of the school district and the individual school buildings at the close of the fiscal year and also examine any related statements of transactions in the various funds for the fiscal year ended.
- Conduct audit in accordance with legal requirements and generally accepted auditing standards.
- Include such audit tests and sampling of the accounting records and other auditing procedures as necessary, and investigate in the level of depth required by the existing circumstances.
- Render an opinion on the state of the financial statements prepared at the close of the fiscal year.
- Prepare such financial statements for publications as required by law and, perhaps, by additional board of education policies.
- Make recommendations to the board of education concerning its accounting records, procedures, and related activities to improve those procedures, records, and activities.
- Provide the superintendent of schools with a confidential letter indicating specific suggestions for improving the fiscal operations conducted by the school district and by its individual school sites. In some cases, specific school building sites may be identified for corrective action; sometimes specific areas, such as student activity accounts, may be identified for corrective action.

In addition, the internal auditor can serve the school district and its constituent school building sites by continuously performing the following activities [14]:

- Determine whether or not all financial transactions for each account within each fund has been recorded accurately and whether they have been recorded under the appropriately coded budgetary accounts and funds.

- Determine whether or not all budget transfers or changes of accounts have been computed and recorded accurately.
- Verify the prices, quantities, and receipts of purchased goods and services and make certain that the appropriate procedures and proofs exist related to the purchased goods.
- Verify that the work of approving, requesting, and recording each financial transaction has been divided among various employees to ensure that each employee's part of the transaction is checked by the work of at least one other employee.
- Verify that the school system and individual school building site journals, registers, ledgers, and financial reports are safeguarded to prevent loss or unauthorized alterations of their contents [15].

Now that we have discussed the entire cyclical budget process, let's review a series of forms that are used by the budget manager(s) at the school building site. Figure 3.6 illustrates an activity account ledger.

Next is an illustration of a school building site's purchase order. It appears in Figure 3.7.

An illustration of a school building site's check request is presented in Figure 3.8.

A school building site's accounts payable form is illustrated in Figure 3.9.

An illustration of a school building site's contract for services form appears in Figure 3.10.

Figure 3.11 illustrates a school building site's supplemental pay form.

Next is a school building site's self-employment agreement form. It is illustrated in Figure 3.12.

Next are copies of the forms used to register and control the accuracy activities related to athletic events. They are illustrated by Figures 3.13, 3.14, 3.15, and 3.16.

Now that we have presented the forms a local school building site uses to control and account for financial matters related to activity events, it is wise to discuss one other area where many schools are often cited for inaccurate accounting. The petty cash fund is an area where it is very important to control expenditure and to accurately account for expenditures [16]. This form is displayed in Figure 3.17.

Date: _____					
Account #	Beginning Balance	Ending Receipts	Disbursements	Transfer	Balance
100 Field trip	270.45	00	00	00	270.45
148 Inst. supplies					
students	210.25	00	00	00	210.25
538 Donations PTA	3,350.00	00	00	00	3,350.00
673 Interest	192.65	00	00	00	192.65
678 Miscellaneous	120.00	00	00	00	120.00
769 Vending drinks	400.50	00	00	00	400.50
830 Performing arts	00	00	00	00	00
TOTALS:	4,543.85	00	00	00	4,543.85
Account #					
990 Petty cash	00	00	00	00	00
991 Cash on hand	00	00	00	00	00
992 Union Bank					
#12543	4,386.87	00	00	00	4,386.87
993 Federal Bank					
#679810	156.98	00	00	00	156.98
994 Investments	00	00	00	00	00
999 Activity transfers	00	00	00	00	00
TOTALS:	4,543.85	00	00	00	4,543.85

Figure 3.6 *School building site's activity account ledger.*

DATE: _____	SHIP TO: _____	
	(Name and address of school building)	
_____ _____ (Name and address of supplier) TERMS OF PAYMENT: 30 DAYS NET	NOTE: Schools are tax exempt from sales taxes	
Quantity	Unit	Description	Unit Price	Total
1	ea	Hanging map of U.S.	59.75	59.75
3	ea	Workbooks for map	3.00	9.00
			Subtotal:	68.75
			Less: 20%	13.75
			TOTAL:	55.00

Figure 3.7 *School building site's purchase order.*

57

Name of School: _____ Date: _____
Account #: ___769___   Account Name: Vending drinks
Payee Description: Cola for vending machine
Check # ___1162___   Amount: ___15.00___   P.O. # ___248692___   Vendor # 12
Vendor's Name: Cola Bottling Co.
Requested By:_____ Date:_____
(Name)
Approved By:_____ Date:_____
(Principal)

Figure 3.8 *School building site's check request.*

Name of School:_____ Date:_____

Prepared By:_____ Approved By:_____
     (Name)   (Principal)

Vendor	Date of Invoice	Account # for Purchase	P.O. #	Amount	Instruction for Paid Date
Cola Co.	6/14/96	769	124	700.00	Pd. Monthly
Super Store	5/29/96	148	123	14.54	Pd. Monthly
Office Sales	5/28/96	170	122	9.60	Pd. Monthly
				TOTAL: 724.14	

Figure 3.9 *School building site's accounts payable form.*

58

```
CONTRACT #:_____  DATE:_____
SCHOOL:_____
CONTRACTOR: ABC AMBULANCE CO.
SERVICES TO BE PERFORMED: ABC Ambulance Company will provide on-site
service for eight (8) football games for Exemplary High School at a cost of $125.00
per game. Payment will be paid upon receipt of an invoice at the end of the last game
of the season.
DATES OF SERVICE: From August 15, 1996 through November 16, 1996.
TOTAL CONTRACT AMOUNT: $1,000.00
CONTRACTOR:_____  Principal:_____
              (Signature)                    (Signature)
DATE:_____            DATE:_____
```

Figure 3.10 *School building site's contract for services form.*

Explanation: Extra Clerical Days   Charge Code: 10-1109-011-100

Principal:_____ Date:_____

Employee Name and Soc. Sec. No.	Dates Served Some/To	Daily/Hourly Hours Worked	No. Days Worked	Total Pay
1. Jane Doe 132-48-6894	3-16/3-18	47.00	3	141.00
2.				
3.				

Figure 3.11 *School building site's supplemental pay form.*

Date:_____ School:_____

Name:_____ SSN#:_____

Address:_____

_____

If Regular Employee, List Regular Employment Title:_____

Date(s) Worked:_____

Types of Services Performed:_____

Check Amount:_____ Account No.:_____ Check No.:_____

I, the undersigned agree to the accuracy of the above information.

_____   _____
        (Contractor's Signature)   (Principal of Other Authorized Signature)

Figure 3.12 School building site's self-employment agreement form. (This form is used to pay for employees who perform duties as ticket sellers/takers for athletic events and for nonemployees who perform such contractual services as speakers and consultants.)

Date of Game:_____ Name of School:_____

Home Team:_____ Name of Sport:_____

Visiting Team:_____ Location of Game:_____

Tickets Issued To:_____ Ticket Color:_____

Check One: Pregame Sales __X__ Gate Sales_____ Ticket Price $4.00

Signatures:

Ticket Seller:_____ Date:_____

Gate Supervisor:_____ Date:_____

Ticket #s Issued	Last Ticket Sold	First Ticket Sold	Total Number Tickets Sold	Total Sales
101	1168	101	1068	$4,272.00

Note: This form is to be completed by the gate supervisor in the presence of the ticket seller.

I, the undersigned affirm that the signatures above are bona fide.

_____ Date:_____
        (Principal or Athletic Director)

Figure 3.13 School building site's ticket report form.

School:	Game: Science Tech. High vs. Mentor High
Date:	Stadium:

A. Ticket Sales
   1. Presales $2,887.00
   2. Gate sales   394.00
   3. Reserved   .00
   4. Overage/shortage   (.15)
      Total Ticket Sales: $3,270.85
B. Expenses
   1. Police   (six × $40.00) $240.00
   2. Gate worker   (five × $18.00)   90.00
   3. Clock operator   (one × $00)   .00
   4. Public address operator   (one × $25.00)   25.00
   5. Police   (four × $00)   .00
   6. Doctor   (one × $00)   .00
   7. Ambulance   (one × $200) $200.00
   8. Transportation   .00
   9. Sales tax on tickets sold   88.51
  10. Referees   (four X $200) $800.00
      Total Expenses: $1,443.51
C. Net Income $1,827.34

Figure 3.14 *School building site's athletic financial report form.*

School:	Event Date:	Ticket Color:
Principal:		Date:
(Signature)		

Date Logged Out	Beginning Ticket # Issued	Beginning Ticket # Returned	Type of Ticket	Event Description
9/16/96	17201	17303	Adult	Football

Figure 3.15 *School building site's ticket control log.*

Currency			
# of Bills	Denomination	Total	
1530	$1.00	$1,530.00	
200	5.00	1,000.00	
20	10.00	200.00	
5	20.00	100.00	
0	50.00	.00	
0	100.00	.00	
		Total Currency: $2,830.00	

Coins

# of Rolls	Denomination	Value	
3	Pennies	$1.50	
1	Nickels	2.00	
10	Quarters	50.00	
10	Half Dollars	100.00	
		Total of Rolls: $153.50	

Loose Coins

	Pennies	$.49
	Nickels	1.71
	Quarters	4.80
	Half Dollars	9.50
	Total Loose Coins:	$16.50

Total Cash: $3,000.00   Change Fund: $1,000.00   Net Revenue: $2,000.00

Figure 3.16 *School building site's cash tally/concession revenues report form.*

Amount of Receipts and/or Invoices:	$23.50	
Cash on Hand:	$51.50	
TOTAL: Established Amount of Fund	$75.00	
Prepared by: _____		Date:_____
(Petty Cash Custodian's Signature)		
Approved by: _____		Date:_____
(Principal's Signature)		

THIS FORM AND THE ORIGINAL SUPPORTING DOCUMENTATION MUST BE ATTACHED TO THE LOCAL SCHOOL'S CHECK REQUEST FOR REPLENISHING THE FUND.

Figure 3.17 *School building site's petty cash reconciliation report form.*

A FINAL WORD

We can place an umbrella over the process of school site-based budgeting by mentioning the four basic functions involved: (1) income and resource generation, (2) allocation concepts, (3) expenditure concepts, and (4) management concepts [17].

Income and Resource Generation

Basic school district income is generated by a combination of (1) federal funds (earmarked or block grant), (2) state funds (state aid that is earmarked and/or block grants, along with flow-through funds from the federal government, and local funds (property taxes, sales taxes, etc.). Occasionally, certain districts will derive funds from taxes on liquor, tobacco, or gambling and other earmarked funds.

The building level will derive its allocation of funds from the district level. The school building can increase its resources by successfully applying for grants, by persuading a business partner to adopt the school, and by a variety of fund-raising activities. In addition, the school can solicit gifts of equipment and/or supplies from the community at large. Also, the school building can increase its resources by charging fees for school events, and some schools can charge student fees for books or supplies. The school building can operate a profitable school store (frequently the case in large middle or high schools). Finally, the school building can invest funds until they are needed, thereby gaining interest on these investments [18].

Allocation Concepts

When dealing with the allocation of resources, the decision makers should consider the concepts of human capital, cost/benefit analysis, and cost-effectiveness analysis. (1) Human capital is a concept that allows decision makers to project the degree of improvement that will be attained by students and employees by the investment of available funds and of employee time and effort. Obviously, alternative expenditures will be analyzed to maximize the result of investment that produces the greatest growth in human capital. (2) Cost/benefit analysis is a concept that determines the ratio between the cost of a program expenditure to the benefit received by students or employees. If the benefit is predicted to exceed the cost, the program is given the go-ahead to become operational [19]. However, if the cost is predicted to exceed the benefit, then the program is dropped from consideration and other alternative program expenditures are considered. (3) Cost-effectiveness analysis is a concept that is utilized to predict, from a variety of expenditure alternatives, the least expensive way to obtain the desired results of a program [20].

Expenditure Concepts

There are two important expenditure concepts to be considered by the school building decision makers. They are expenditure planning and fairness of expenditures. (1) Expenditure planning involves purchasing with economies of scale and volume purchasing advantages in mind, collecting all potential discounts by paying on time, and combining with other schools to purchase large lots of supplies and other required instructional tools. (2) Fairness of expenditures involves the school building planners giving consideration to the concept of equity [21]. These decision makers should ask questions such as the following: Are all students and employees treated fairly when money is allocated for expenditures? Are some areas receiving a disproportionate amount of available dollars for expenditures—for example, sports, band, or vocational programs? Is there a defensible rationale when expenditures are not equal between and among programs—for example, special education, kindergarten, and science programs?

When answering these questions one must remember that *equity* does not mean *equal* expenditures. It costs more additional dollars for equipment and supplies for a science laboratory program than it does to offer a standard English program with an equal number of students. Also, it costs more to operate a special education classroom than a normal fifth grade classroom because of the smaller number of students enrolled in special education classes. These types of considerations must be thoroughly thought through by the school building's decision makers when considering the fairness of expenditures.

Management Concepts

Management concepts include the matters of (1) predictions, (2) needs assessments, (3) budgeting, (4) expenditure controls, (5) accounting, and (6) auditing.

Predictions

Predicting the number of students who will attend the school in subsequent years is crucial to managing an effective and efficient school building operation. In addition, based upon the number of students and the instructional and other programs to be offered by the school, it is also crucial to predict each category of employee required and the number of employees required within each category. Finally, it is important to project the types and numbers of equipment and supplies required to operate the school building's programs in future years.

Needs Assessment

Needs assessments should be routinely conducted to determine those items where a need exists. Remember that a need is a gap or discrepancy between what is and what should or could be. Once the needs are identified, they should be listed in priority order, and expenditures should be made on the basis of these priorities within the available fund allocations.

Budgeting

Budgeting is the process of planning for the income to be received, the programs to be offered, and the expenditures to be made to operate an effective and efficient school building.

Expenditure Controls

Expenditure controls involve the official designation of those persons who have the authority to expend every fund. Also some person, usually the building principal, should be responsible for the monitoring of expenditures on the basis of allocation, expenditures, encumbrances, and unencumbered funds available at any point in time. This information should be shared with all those official budget managers within the school building to make certain that any necessary adjustments are made on a timely basis to avoid the overexpenditure of budget amounts.

Accounting

A good accounting system will include legality, accuracy, completeness, currency, simplicity, and uniformity. *Legality* implies that all expenditures were legally made, including the transfer of funds from one budget account to another.

Accuracy implies that all income and expenditures from every budget account were entered in a totally accurate manner. *Completeness* implies that every income received and every expenditure disbursed was completely recorded in the account books, including those for the student activity funds.

Currency implies that all income received and all expenditures disbursed are entered into the appropriate accounts at the exact time of receipt or expenditure of funds. If items are delayed beyond the time of receipt or expenditure, errors will increase with the increase in the length of time from the budget action to the time of posting the transactions.

Simplicity implies that the structure for expenditures and accounting for them is easily understood. This is especially important for student activity funds. Student organizations should have an official employee to sign purchase orders and should designate one person to receive funds and another person to deposit funds. The forms used for this purpose should be as simple as possible.

Uniformity implies that all accounts and procedures will be identical and that all budget journal entries into each account will be identically registered.

Auditing

Auditing is a process that inspects and reviews all income received and expenditures made by the budget manager(s) of the local school building. An auditor usually samples the accounts but goes into every account entry if there is a suspicious or illegal activity, mismanagement, or inconsistency of records. Although the school district may have an internal auditor, and it will definitely have an external auditor hired to yearly check on all district level and building level procedures, it is wise for each school building representative to appoint someone to perform periodic audits of the school income and expenditure records. The suggestion of a school building level audit is especially significant for large secondary schools that have a wide variety of extracurricular activities and students activity funds [22].

EXERCISES

(1) Develop a budget calendar.
(2) Determine who shall be included as the responsible budget management persons at the local school building site.

(3) Determine how you would conduct a needs assessment and also determine who you would involve in the needs assessment process.

(4) Develop a system for projecting student enrollments for future years.

(5) Decide upon the criteria you would use to determine the allocation of funds among the various instructional programs at the local school building site. Remember that this should be done in a manner that promotes equality, equity, cost/benefit, and cost effectiveness.

(6) Develop a series of forms that you would use to record the financial transactions, including those for student activity funds, of a local school building site.

REFERENCES

1. Drake, T. L. and W. H. Roe. 1994. *School Business Management: Supporting Instructional Effectiveness.* Boston: Allyn & Bacon, pp. 53–61.
2. Herman, J. J. 1995. *Effective School Facilities: A Development Guidebook.* Technomic Publishing Company, pp. 19, 87.
3. Castetter, W. B. 1996. *The Human Resource Function in Educational Administration.* 6th ed. Englewood Cliffs, NJ: Merrill, pp. 57–60.
4. Odden, A. R. and L. O. Picus. 1992. *School Finance: A Policy Perspective.* New York: McGraw-Hill, p. 303.
5. Burrup, P. E., V. Brimley, Jr., and R. R. Garfield. 1993. *Financing Education in a Climate of Change.* 5th ed. Boston: Allyn & Bacon, pp. 433–439.
6. Rebore, W. T. and R. W. Rebore. 1993. *Introduction to Financial and Business Administration in Public Education.* Boston: Allyn & Bacon, p. 5.
7. Kaufman, R., J. J. Herman, and K. Watters. 1996. *Educational Planning: Strategic, Tactical, Operational.* Lancaster, PA: Technomic Publishing Co., pp. 76–77.
8. Wagner, I. D. and S. M. Sniderman. 1984. *Budgeting School Dollars: A Guide to Spending and Saving,* pp. 197–199.
9. Association of School Business Officials International. 1986. *Internal Audit Guide for Student Activity Funds,* Reston, VA: pp. 13–14.
10. Drake, T. L. and W. H. Roe. *School Business Management.* pp. 119–122.
11. *Ibid.,* pp. 119–145.
12. Burrup, P. E., V. Brimley, Jr., and R. R. Garfield. *Financing Education,* pp. 344–352.
13. Rebore, W. T. and R. W. Rebore. *Introduction,* pp. 147–150.
14. Jordan, K. F., M. P. McKeown, R. G. Salmon, and L. D. Webb. 1985. *School Business Administration.* Newbury Park, CA: Sage Publications, pp. 208–209.
15. Wagner, I. D. and S. M. Sniderman. *Budgeting School Dollars.* pp. 136–142.
16. Jordan, K. F., M. P. McKeown, R. G. Salmon, and L. D. Webb. *School Business Administration,* pp. 196–197.
17. Drake, T. L. and W. H. Roe. *School Business Management,* pp. 78–83.

18. Rebore, W. T. and R. W. Rebore. *Introduction,* pp. 167–178.

19. Wagner, I. D. and S. M. Sniderman. 1984. *Budgeting School Dollars.* pp. 239–241.

20. Brown, D. J. 1995. "The Sabotage of School-Based Management." *School Administrator,* 52 (3): 8–12.

21. Kearney, K. A. 1992. "Marketing Your Budget." *American School Board Journal,* 179 (8): 41.

22. Drake, T. L. and W. H. Roe. *School Business Management,* pp. 91–116.

School Site-Based Budgeting: A Case Study

CHAPTER 4 PRESENTS a comprehensive case study of the methodologies and forms utilized by a school district in Michigan. The fictitious name of Comprehensive School District will be used so that the district's school sites are kept confidential. The chapter ends with a final word, exercises, and a series of appendices.

Comprehensive School District has 6,035 students. It has one high school, two middle schools, and five elementary schools. The senior high school houses 2,150 students, the two middle schools each house approximately 800 students, and the five elementary schools have approximately the same number of students housing the remaining 3,085 students.

A FUTURE-ORIENTED COMPREHENSIVE NEEDS ASSESSMENT

The example begins with the actual involvement of more than 400 citizens, employees, and students in a needs assessment process, with the needs to be arrayed over a future five-year period on the basis of the priority levels established by the needs assessment committees.

Each school building in the district had a needs assessment committee consisting of a minimum of twenty parents and citizens, two teachers; two classified employees; the building principal; and one assistant principal in large student body schools; and at the secondary school level four students. In addition, the district organized committees of similar composition to study each functional area (administration, finance, business, personnel, instruction, building and grounds, transportation, athletics, music, clubs, food services, custodial services, maintenance services) and any other area that the district steering committee felt would be worthy of investigation [1]. For example, the district steering committee added a subcommittee to investigate investments of the school district.

Arriving at the Needs List

It must be emphasized that a need is a gap or discrepancy between what is and what should or could be [2]. It is not a wish list or a wants list that the district and building planning committees were charged with investigating and identifying—it was a needs list.

This needs assessment process began when the board of education approved a strategic planning process that involved developing a comprehensive needs list that was to become the focus of action for a five-year period into the future. The board also approved the creation and the membership of the district planning committee and all the school building level and district functional levels subcommittees.

The charge given each committee was to investigate and determine every need of the specific building for which it served as the needs assessment committee or the district functional area for which it was appointed. The board of education's charge indicated that, at this juncture, the committee was not to concern itself with the cost of any or all of the needs; a cost estimate would be computed later for each need the committee identified [3]. Also, all needs should be identified that would make the schools of the district the best that they could possibly become. The board of education also charged the committee to present a written and oral report at a regularly scheduled public board meeting in June of the school year.

In addition, the committee members were to appoint a chairperson, a vice chairperson, and a recorder. A central office administrator was assigned as liaison, and it was this person's task to arrange for all the meeting site details and for the recording, printing, and distribution of the committee's deliberations and actions. The central office public relations official was responsible for keeping the media informed of the process and decisions, and a newsletter detailing the status of the needs assessment process and the decisions that were being made was sent to every home in the school district on a biweekly basis [4].

After a full school year of investigation, each committee had an extensive list of needs it felt would improve each school and each school district function. The list contained more than 500 needs.

After the board of education thoroughly reviewed the mass of needs identified that were intended to make the schools the best they could possibly be, it requested that each committee appoint two of its members, with one having to be a parent or citizen, to review the total list of identified needs from all committees and to place the total needs in priority.

Once this was completed, the prioritizing committee was asked to schedule the needs over a five-year time period. This task was completed during the summer months.

It was up to this committee to decide whether new kindergarten equipment was more important than a wrestling mat; or whether hiring additional teacher aides was more important than initiating an international baccalaureate program at the high school; or whether the construction of a new science lab was more important than increasing the field trip budgets for the elementary schools; or whether the addition of Russian and Japanese language instruction to the middle school curriculum was more important than establishing a local area network (LAN) to connect the central district's and individual school buildings' computers. Many other similar decisions had to be made.

Once the prioritized needs were submitted to the board of education, the board of education charged the central and building level administration to cost out each identified need. This task took approximately three additional months. The board then reviewed all the prioritized recommendations and the costs associated with each and worked with the employees to develop recommended action programs to meet the identified needs for the first year, with the promise to continue this process for each of the five years [5]. The final decisions made by the board involved four specific types of actions; examples of each type will suffice to illustrate the actions taken on each type. Throughout this process, every action was taken at open, public, preannounced official board meetings, and an informational newsletter continued to be distributed to each home.

An example of the method of the board's official response to each identified need will suffice to explain the actions taken. In each case, the entire community was informed by the school district's newsletter and coverage by the area media of the final official action taken by the board of education.

(1) The need was not approved. An example of this result was when some elementary schools expressed a need to add a strings program to the music offerings. The board refused this identified need, indicating that the instrumental and vocal music was offered at the elementary level, but strings would continue to be offered at the middle school and senior high school levels. However, the board directed the director of community education to establish a strings tutoring program for elementary level students, and to do so for a nominal fee.

(2) The need was approved and a specific action program was detailed. An example of this need was when the middle school needs assessment committees expressed the need to increase funds for environmental field trips and study. The board directed the assistant superintendent for instruction and the director of transportation to work with the middle school teachers and the middle school principals to develop a specific plan. Once the plan was developed, the board then directed the assistant superintendent for business to take the necessary funds out of existing accounts and transfer them to an account for this purpose.

(3) The need was approved and immediate program and/or budget adjustments were made to implement the action program to resolve and meet the identified and approved need. An example of this need was the identified need for new marching band uniforms. Funding was accomplished by transferring the required amount of money from budget accounts meant for other purchases.

(4) The need was approved but it would be acted upon only if the district's voters approved additional millage to fund the identified and approved need. An example was the identified need to remodel and add an addition to one of the district's elementary school building. Another example was the need to add a comprehensive summer program, free of fees to the students. All of these types of needs were listed on a tax referendum because they could not be accommodated within the normal yearly budget allocations.

Determining the Cost of the Identified Needs

After all the needs were identified, the superintendent and the rest of the district's administrators went about the task of projecting the cost of each of the identified needs for each of the five years into the future. This process took approximately three months, and a report was given to the board at a publicly called special meeting.

The Board of Education's Actions Related to Each Identified Need

The official board actions were heavily covered by the media and the school district's newsletter, indicating the total identified needs for five years and the cost of each need. Subsequently, three additional official publicly announced board of education meetings were held to discuss all the needs and their costs, and the board of education took action on each of the needs. After each meeting, the public again received a report of the board's official actions.

The final decisions made by the board involved four specific types of actions: examples of each type (shown previously) illustrate the actions taken on each type. Throughout this process, every action was taken at public, preannounced official board of education meetings, and an informational newsletter was distributed to each home.

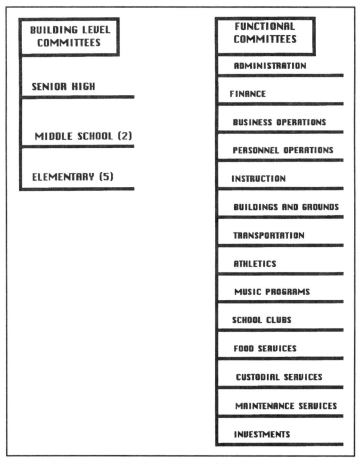

Figure 4.1 *Comprehensive School District's needs assessment structure.*

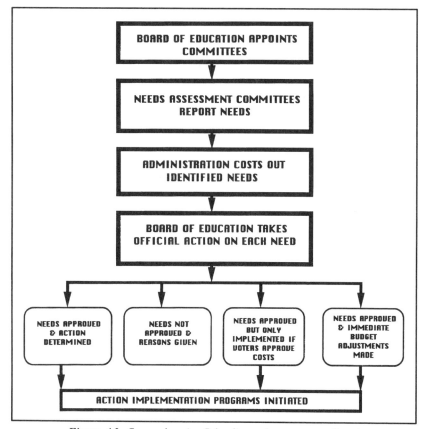

Figure 4.2 *Comprehensive School's needs assessment flowchart.*

Many other items that would cause an increase in the school district's operational millage were also put to a vote of the residents of the school district. In most cases, these were items submitted as identified priorities by individual school building needs assessment committees, but they could not be implemented within the existing income available to the school district. In each case, the projected cost of these items was listed, and those that were voted upon favorably by the school district's voters were implemented.

Dealing with the Noncost Identified Needs

Some of the identified needs had no dollar cost associated with them.

These needs included some procedures utilized by the district's administrators; and some involved a modification, addition, or removal of board of education's officially adopted policy. Each of these needs was reviewed and some standard operating procedures (SOPs) and some policies were added, deleted, or modified.

At this juncture, it is appropriate to summarize the needs assessment process used by Comprehensive School District. Figure 4.1 illustrates the school district's needs assessment structural dimension. Also, Figure 4.2 illustrates the school district's needs assessment process dimension.

Before the allocation of school building site-based budget funds could be established, the number of pupils to be educated at each school site had to be projected. This student projection joined the needs assessment results as crucial, since the number of teachers, aides, and other categories of employees would be impacted by the number of students attending each school.

PROJECTING THE STUDENT POPULATION
FIVE YEARS INTO THE FUTURE

The methodology utilized for projecting the student population was three-dimensional in nature. First, each school building principal was held responsible for projecting her/his school's student population; second, the central administration utilized the cohort survival method to project the student population for each school attendance area and for the entire school district; and third, based upon past history of projections of each principal and of the central administration, an error factor was determined for each school building's attendance area and for the entire school district.

Figure 4.3 illustrates the cohort survival method of student projections utilized by the school district's central administrative staff [6]. The illustration merely indicates the procedure for grades one and two for a single elementary school. The procedure would be completed for all grades kindergarten through twelve, and it would be done for each school building and for the entire district's totals. The steps are as follows:

(1) Take the actual number of students enrolled in each grade for eleven years.

(2) Figure a ten-year percentage of student survival by dividing the subsequent year's number of students by the previous year's and grade's

SCHOOL YEAR	GRADE ONE		GRADE TWO	
	NUMBER	PERCENT	NUMBER	PERCENT
ACTUAL				
YEAR #1	341		315	XXX
YEAR #2	369		316	92.7
YEAR #3	368		338	91.6
YEAR #4	348		351	95.4
YEAR #5	344		289	85.8
YEAR #6	328		287	83.4
YEAR #7	329		300	91.5
YEAR #8	307		292	88.8
YEAR #9	382		382	98.4
YEAR #10	349		393	107.8
YEAR #11	375		325	93.8
FUTURE		MEAN PERCENTAGE=	92.7	
YEAR #1	345		348	(year #11 x 92.7%)
YEAR #2	338		328	(future Year #1 x 92.7)
YEAR #3	333		313	
YEAR #X	379		389	

Figure 4.3 Cohort survival methodology for projecting student enrollments.

students (for example, divide the second grade number of students for year two by the number of first grade students for year one). Do this for each of ten years and for each grade level.

(3) Compute the mean (average) percentage of survival for the ten historical years.

(4) Multiply that mean percentage of survival against each previous year to determine the number of students in each future year for each grade.

A word of caution is important at this juncture. If there is a change of attendance boundaries, a boom in housing construction, or a rapidly decreasing or increasing pattern of students in the last few of the eleven historical years, a reasonable extrapolation must be made in order to maintain an accuracy in the student projections for future years. Consideration should also be given to the types of new construction starting in a district. The numbers of rental houses, apartments, and mobile home parks will specifically impact the projected numbers of students. This can also be monitored by pursual of new zoning and construction permits, particularly in the attendance areas of each individual building. It is common for established areas or older suburbs to become vacant or lose youth population while different areas of the same district develop new facility needs.

PROJECTING EMPLOYEE REQUIREMENTS FIVE YEARS INTO THE FUTURE

Once the student populations are projected, then the numbers of each category of employee, with their associated salary and fringe benefit costs, can be projected. In each case, an estimate of the changes caused by increased health insurance, union/management negotiated contracts, and general cost of doing business related to employees has to be determined.

PROJECTING INCOME REQUIREMENTS FIVE YEARS INTO THE FUTURE

Once the identified needs have been determined, the number of students projected, the number of each category of employee required has been identified, and the other expenditures of operating the schools have been determined, a cost estimate for operating the schools can be made. Once that cost estimate is projected, the amount of income required to operate the school can be determined. If the projected costs are within the income estimate, everything is ready to go. However, if the cost estimates of operating the schools are greater than the estimated income of the school district, operational plans must be scaled down or additional sources of income (such as asking residents to vote additional millage) have to be found.

Now that the initial structure and processes that affect the individual school buildings and the school district level have been illustrated, we turn to the specifics of the relationship between the school district budgeting procedures and the school building site-based budgeting procedures.

COMPREHENSIVE SCHOOL DISTRICT AND SCHOOL SITE-BASED BUDGETING PROCEDURES

Faced with the needs assessment projected over a five-year period and the knowledge of the board action on these needs, the building principals and the central administration annually evaluated and made any necessary or desired modifications to the following procedures. Even though the building principal was the official budget planning and control manager, all involved clearly agreed that the employees and each building's school-based management council was to be involved in all phases of the school building's budgetary deliberations and decisions. The school-based management councils each had a mixture of parents, citizens, teachers, and the principal—numbering from twenty to thirty persons per specific committee [7].

When a district is planning its budget, the budget managers are living with the current year's funds while planning for the subsequent year's budget. This planning is best controlled by the development and utilization of a budget calendar. Comprehensive School District's annual budget methodology and planning calendar is presented in Figure 4.4.

Once the budget calendar is finalized, a copy of the methodological directions and clarifications is distributed to all administrators to be used with their building of central employees and with the building school-based management councils. It should be noted that all procedures, employee ratios, and dollar allocations are reviewed and updated by all principals and central office administrators over a two-week period during each summer. A copy of the directions and clarifications distributed is presented in Figure 4.5. All forms indicated are placed as appendices at the end of this book.

Also, specific examples demonstrating how to compute the formulas were included to help those who required this assistance. Figures 4.6, 4.7, and 4.8 show three specific examples: (1) a staff conversion table; (2) a weighted pupil formula; and (3) actual school building examples for the senior high, a middle school, and an elementary school. (The actual dollar amount per 1.000 staff equivalency is adjusted each year at the summer workshop.)

Target Date	Task	Form	Person(s) Responsible
1st day of school year	Predicted student count & actual student count	None	Principals
1st month's 4th Friday	Listing of number of students enrolled in each class section	None	Principals (copies to superintendent)
October 15	Student population predictions for subsequent year	Form W	Principals and assistant superintendents
4th Friday of each month	Monthly actual pupil count	Form WW	Principals (copies to superintendent)
4th Friday of each month	Log of students entering and leaving	Form WX	Principals (copies to superintendent)
October 15	Staff equivalency summary requests	Form X-1	All administrators
October 20	Actual total employee printout	Data Printout	Assistant sup't. for personnel (copies to all administrators)
October 30	Student population predictions finalized	Form W	Superintendent to report in actual and weighted for staffing purposes (copies to all administrators)
November 1	All itinerant schedules finalized	None	Assistant sup't. for instruction (copies to all administrators)
November 1	All summer school staff finalized	None	Principals & assistant sup't. for instruction
November 15	All staff requests including (a) cocurricular (b) curriculum funds at 1.0 equivalency per $25,000, (c) summer extended year contracts at 1.0 equivalency (d) equipment and supply transfers at 1.0 equivalency	Data printout, Form X and Form X-1	(a) All admin. use separate form X for each budget account (b) All administrators (c) Assistant sup't. for personnel (d) Principals all transfers noted on Form X and a written explanation to the sup't. Also, Form Y entries noted
November 30	Staff requests finalized by budget code and building location	Form X-1	Superintendent with advice of all administrators
November 30	Budget requests based on needs assessment listed in priority order with costs & rationale	Forms Y, Z and Z-1	Principals and all administrators (copies to superintendent and Ass't. sup't for business)

Figure 4.4 Comprehensive School District's budget methodology and planning calendar.

Target Date	Task	Form	Person(s) Responsible
December 15	Staff requests presented to board or education for approval	None	Superintendent
December 26–28	Budget requests finalized	Forms Y, Z and Z-1	All building principals and central admin. daily 9–4 P.M. workshop
January 15	Total tentative budget completed, including income and expenditure estimates and site budgets identified	None	Assistant sup't for business (copies to all administrators)
February 15	Tentative budget presented to the board of education	None	Superintendent
March 15	Tentative budget modified if board of education makes changes	None	Board of education (superintendent makes these changes)
May 15	Double check on accuracy and update all information	None	Principals and all administrators
May 30	Public hearing on budget	None	Board of education and all admin.
June 15	Finalized subsequent year's budget presented and formally approved by board of education	None	Superintendent and all administrators present budget, board of education approves budget, ass't. sup't. for business produces and distributes to all administrators, media and SBM councils
Any time after June 15	Personnel change requests	Form XX	All administrators
Any time after June 15	Budget expenditure change requests	Form ZZ	All administrators

NOTATIONS:

1. Any changes in priorities, requested over expenditures, transfer of expenditures from one budget code to another, or similar requests are to be filed on a ZZ Form after May 15.
2. Any changes of staff requests or staff assignment changes are to be filed on a XX Form after May 15.
3. There are three budget reviews planned for: (a) after 4th Friday of first month of school, (b) at mid-year, and (c) in May.

Figure 4.4 (continued) *Comprehensive School District's budget methodology and planning calendar.*

Budget Planning

In order to provide for an appropriate and efficient team effort related to the budget planning process, it is necessary that (a) the written guidelines are carefully followed, (b) all target dates are met by each administrator, and (c) future planning is accomplished in a detailed, accurate, but unhurried manner. Discussions at administrative council meetings are encouraged, and individual and small-group conferences will be arranged, upon request, to clarify any budget item or budget process. It is expected that all administrators will involve their employees in the budget planning process, and all principals will also involve their school-based management (communication and governance) committees in the budget planning process.

NOTE: Funded projects will involve separate budget construction of a programmed nature as dictated by the funding agency in each case.

Guidelines for the Use of Budget Forms

The responsible administrator will be held accountable for completing and forwarding the forms with copies, as indicated in the Budget Planning Calendar, on or prior to the date indicated. It is crucial that individual target dates are met in order that the total budgetary planning procedure is not unnecessarily delayed.

1. Form W: Pupil Population Predictions

   Retain a copy of this form for use if a review of initial estimates is required later in the year. The "actual predicated" and the "weighted" membership columns are both important as the actual is used to predict income on various state and federal formulas, while the weighted is used to determine the staff equivalencies and the unit budget allocations. The estimates, when finalized by the superintendent of schools, will be used for all subsequent staffing and unit budget planning.

2. Form X: Personnel Staffing Request and Form X-1: Summary of Staff

   a. All building principals should report their staff requests utilizing the agreed upon allocation of professional staff equivalencies per 1,000 pupils. In this request format, all building site level format, all administrative, secretarial, clerical, co-op students, aides, summer and added employment at 1.0 equivalents per $20,000; budget transfers for equipment or materials and supplies at 1.0 equivalents per $20,000; and cocurricular activities at 1.0 equivalents per $20,000 are to be included on this form.

   b. As agreed upon at our summer workshop, the principals will exclude from the staff equivalencies, all food service, custodial and maintenance, crossing guard, special education, Title One (and other federal programs), transportation, and district level employees.

   c. The data printout should be used by administrators as a basis to complete new forms with any modifications, additions, subtractions, budget transfers, or corrections indicated on Form X. The printout and the completed Form X will provide the total information with a minimum of effort. Use a separate Form X for each staff account number, and make certain to attach a Form X-1: Summary of Staff form.

   d. The appropriate administrator in charge shall list those staff members who function under specialized funded programs.

Figure 4.5 Comprehensive School District's budget methodology: directions and clarifications.

e. The assistant superintendent for instruction shall list all summer school personnel and shall determine the pro rata staffing assigned each building for itinerant nonspecial education personnel. The assistant superintendent for personnel will list all special education personnel. However, those itinerant positions must be listed by the individual building principals. The pro rata staffing for itinerants shall be determined on a per minute basis (including travel, planning, and lunchtimes).

f. Although great flexibility is granted the building principal within the planning methodology, there shall be no reductions beyond the previous year in foreign language, reading, art, physical education, music, or library/media personnel without PRIOR APPROVAL OF THE SUPERINTENDENT.

g. All nonbuilding-level administrators will report staff requests on all actual numbers of employees needed, not on a professional staff equivalency basis.

h. The district's director of media may make independent media staff requests. The principals must include building-level media staff within her/his allocated professional staff equivalency, although this may not necessarily agree with the requests of the district's director of media.

i. The assistant superintendent for business shall list all business office employees, and the operations manager shall list all custodial, maintenance, food service, and transportation employees.

j. The director of community education shall list all community education employees.

k. The assistant superintendent for personnel shall include (1) all contracted services related to hourly or project related matters where full-time employees are not hired, (2) 2.5 teaching equivalencies shall be added to allow for up to 2% of the bargaining unit's employees to be granted sabbatical leaves (five teachers at one-half pay), and (3) any Elementary Internship Program (EIP) coordinators.

NOTES:

- See the appendices for workday definitions and the conversion table of staff equivalencies (based on 1,000 pupils).

- If an individual staff member is assigned to more than one program (for example: 60% community education and 40% special education), list the name of the employee and the appropriate percentage under each separate account listing.

- Refer to appendices for standard workdays per year for all employees.

3. Form Y: Instructional Expense

As agreed upon at the summer workshop, this form and the amounts listed are to be used to distribute all basic unit budget allocations under the guidelines listed below:

*$44.10 per elementary pupil **($4.39 earmarked for replacement of equipment)

*$49.60 per middle school pupil **($6.96 earmarked for replacement of equipment)

*$54.00 per senior high pupil **($8.40 earmarked for replacement of equipment)

*Where weighting is applicable, the weighted pupil figures are to be utilized.
**May be reduced upon written certification (attached to Form Y) from building principal to the superintendent indicating there is not a necessity to replace existing equipment.

Figure 4.5 (continued) *Comprehensive School District's budget methodology: directions and clarifications.*

In addition, the following computations apply:

$8.60 per elementary pupil for media ($2.66 earmarked for replacement of equipment).

$9.92 per middle school pupil for media ($4.79 earmarked for replacement of equipment).

$12.90 per senior high pupil for media ($6.99 earmarked for replacement of equipment).

$2.53 per elementary pupil for cocurricular.

$15.25 per middle school pupil for athletics and cocurricular.

$30.15 per senior high pupil for athletics and cocurricular.

$496.00 per special education teaching site.

NOTE:

Vocational and other added cost programs shall be provided earmarked added unit budget funds as determined by the payout distribution agreed to by the individual building principal and the assistant superintendent for business, except that new or enlarged programs shall be presented to all the principals and central administrators for approval prior to implementation.

4. Form Z: Educational Program and Other Expenditures

   a. This form is designed for multiple uses to record various types of requests. Form Z is to be used for requesting budget allocations for specific educational program improvements over and above those covered by the basic unit budget allocations. Also, Form Z is used for added allocation requests for special education or other specially funded programs.

   b. Some specific example areas of requests are:

Capital Outlay—New:	Examples:
Buildings	Adding bulletin boards
Grounds	New blacktop area
Equipment	New computers

Major Maintenance (Repair or Replacement):	Examples:
Buildings	Replacement of damaged bulletin bd.
Grounds	Resurfacing blacktop areas
Equipment	Replacing damaged computers

Educational Programs

Professional Conferences

Field Trips—using school district's buses

Unusual Cocurricular (athletic and other) Events

Equipment Maintenance Contracts

Figure 4.5 (continued) *Comprehensive School District's budget methodology: directions and clarifications.*

NOTES:

1. Use a separate page for each major budget category.

2. Put like items (in the same budget code) on single sheets, separated from other budget codes so that they may be easily duplicated.

3. List each item in priority by ranking it by letter and numerical ran. Examples are: A-1, A-2, A-3, B-1, B-2, B-3, B-4, C-1, C-2, C-3, C-4, D-1, D-2, D-3, D-4. Following are the definitions related to these letter codes.

A—Necessary is required before September. (Examples: supplies to begin school year, furniture for added students).

B—Effective is required for an effective educational program, and is needed as early in the school year as possible (examples: computer software, videotapes).

C—Excellence is desired for improvement. To be allocated after priority A and B items have been provided, and if funds are available (examples: to begin a totally new educational program, added environmental field trips related to existing science program offerings).

D—Future/Creativity may be unique, and probability of normal funding is remote. Worthy of a foundation grant, a gift, or a federal grant for innovation.

The numerical rank indicates the identified needs within the lettered priority system.

5. Form Z-1: Summary of Z Form Requests

Each budget manager is to summarize the requests for capital outlay, maintenance or added programs beyond the unit budget allocated on Form Z-1 in a manner that groups each request by A, B, C, D priorities.

6. Form CC

This form is to be used for any desired change in the number or assignment of employees (including those on hold status) after the original approval date. The superintendent must approve any change beyond the date of initial finalization.

7. Form ZZ

This form is to be used for any desired change in amount, program or priority that is requested after final agreement is reached. The superintendent must approve any change beyond the date of finalization.

NOTE:

In completing each form, refer to your copy of account numbers for your budget categories.

Figure 4.5 (continued) Comprehensive School District's budget methodology: directions and clarifications.

Category of Personnel		Staff Equivalency
1. Teacher		1.000
2. Administrator		2.000
3. Curriculum development per $20,000		1.000
4. Cocurricular staff per $20,000 (specific amounts of ratios and nonathletic cocurricular sponsors match the dollar amounts in the negotiated union contracts)		1.000
5. Summer and added work day or year for staff employment per $20,000		1.000
6. Budget transfer for equipment or supplies per $20,000		1.000
7. Secretary/clerical equivalency		
Total paid days per year (includes holidays and paid vacations)		
260 days at 7.5 hours		.500
250		.481
240		.462
230		.442
220		.423
208		.400
195		.375
189		.364
8. Aides and students working in the office		
Total paid days per year (includes holidays and paid vacations where applicable)		
193 days at	8 hours per day	.396
193	7 hours	.346
193	6 hours	.297
193	5 hours	.247
193	4 hours	.198
193	3 hours	.148
193	2 hours	.099
193	1 hour	.045
187 days at 8 hours per day (includes holidays and paid vacations where applicable)		
187 days at	8 hours per day	.384
187	7 hours	.336
187	6 hours	.288
187	5 hours	.240
187	4 hours	.192
187	3 hours	.144
187	2 hours	.096
187	1 hour	.048

Figure 4.6 Staff conversion tables to be used in determining staff equivalencies per 1,000 pupils.

Elementary:

The student weighting shall be 114.0% of the actual predicted membership. It is computed as follows (this excludes required staff time prior to and subsequent to the student day, lunch period, etc.):

$$
\begin{array}{rl}
1{,}800 & \text{minutes per week of student instruction} \\
-225 & \text{minutes staff planning time required by union contract} \\
\hline
1{,}575 & \text{teachers minutes with students} \\
\times .14\% \\
\hline
220.50 \\
+1{,}575.00 \\
\hline
=1{,}795.50 & \text{minutes per week}
\end{array}
$$

Middle School:

The student weighting shall be 116.7% of the actual predicted membership. It is computed as follows (this excludes required staff time prior to and subsequent to the student day, lunch period, etc.)

$$
\begin{array}{rl}
7 & \text{periods per day per student instruction} \\
6 & \text{periods per day per teacher instruction} \\
\hline
1/6 & \text{or } 16.7\% \text{ adjustment}
\end{array}
$$

Senior High:

The student weighting shall be .20% for each class taken. This is due to the fact that a full student load is 6 classes, while the teachers are only required to instruct 5 class periods (this excludes required staff time prior to and subsequent to the student day, lunch period, etc.). It is also modified for vocational education students, mid year graduation, and part-time students. The total weighting is computed as follows:

1. Students taking

   6 hours = 1.20 × no. of students = weighting
   5 hours = 1.00
   4 hours = .80
   3 hours = .60
   2 hours = .40
   1 hour = .20

2. The number of students attending area vocational school divided by 2 = weighting

3. Actual = 1st semester and 2nd semester enrollments divided by 2 minus deducts indicated above, plus adds indicated above = actual and weighted students for staffing and unit budget planning purposes.

Figure 4.7 Pupil weighting formulas to be used for staffing and basic unit budget planning purposes.

A. Senior High

1st semester enrollment	9th	10th	11th	12th	Actual Totals
6 hours	478	491	203	99	1,271
5 hours	1	3	291	340	635
4 hours	0	0	0	13	13
3 hours	0	0	0	2	2
2 hours	0	0	0	0	0
1 hour	0	0	0	0	0
TOTAL:	479	494	494	454	1,921

2nd semester enrollment	9th	10th	11th	12th	Actual Totals
6 hours	472	480	154	45	1,151
5 hours	0	2	329	82	413
4 hours	0	0	0	109	109
3 hours	0	0	0	101	101
2 hours	0	0	0	40	40
1 hour	0	0	0	9	9
TOTAL:	472	482	483	386	1,823

Mean = 1st = 2nd divided by 2

	9th	10th	11th	12th	Totals
Actual =	476	489	489	421	1,875
Weighted =	571	586	525	386	2,068

Subtracts from weighting

```
                                            2,068  weighted students
Vocational Area Center 80 students divided by 2 =  − 40  students
Total weighted for staffing:                2,028  students
```

1. High school staff equivalency computation at 50 staff equivalencies per 1,000 pupils:

   Actual = 1,875 students on yearly average
   Note: 1,921 students actual first semester count to be used for income purposes

   Weighted = 1,994 students to be used for staffing and unit budget allocations for 1996 year 1996 at 50 staff equivalency per 1,000 pupils = 99.70 staff equivalencies

   This staff equivalency formula includes all professional staff except: (1) cocurricular, (2) administration, (3) secretaries, (4) clerks, (5) aides, and (6) co-op students at the weightings listed, (7) all added summer or other employment beyond the normal schedule, (8) all curriculum planning at 1.0 staffing per $20,000, and (9) all equipment and supplies at 1.0 staff equivalency per $20,000 budget transfer.

2. High school staff equivalency computation at 53 staff equivalencies per 1,000 pupils:

   1,994 × 53 per 1,000 = 105.68 staff equivalencies
   This equivalency formula includes all the above variables, plus 2.0 for each administrator and 1.0 for $20,000 cocurricular.

Figure 4.8 *Examples of the formula weights in operation, based upon actual information.*

B. Middle School

Middle school staff equivalency computation at 50 staff equivalencies per 1,000 pupils:

692 actual pupils × 116.7% weighted = 807 pupils
.807 × 50 = 40.35 staff equivalencies

C. Elementary

Elementary staff equivalency computation at 52 staff equivalencies per 1,000 pupils:

452 actual pupils
− 40 (80 1/2-day kdgn students)
412 × 114% weighted = 470 weighted pupils
.470 × 52 = 24.44 staff equivalencies

NOTATIONS:

1. Additional base unit budget will be increased as the weighted pupil count will be used for this purpose instead of the actual pupil count.

2. Base unit budget will include the basic allocation from the unit budget and any switch offs.

3. For the budget computation for unit budget allocations use the following for 1996:

Allocations

Elementary School: 52 staff equivalencies per 1,000 weighted pupils

Middle School: 53 staff equivalencies per 1,000 weighted pupils

Senior High School: 54 staff equivalencies per 1,000 weighted pupils

Note: Itemize your staff requests of Form X for the base allocation. Also, list the added staff equivalencies for alternative allocations, and add a written rationale statement related to the educational value(s) expected from the alternative allocation.

Figure 4.8 (continued) Examples of the formula weights in operation, based upon actual information.

ACCOUNTABILITY AND CONTROL PROCEDURES

Zero-sum budgeting is a process that allows for in-process changes in budget expenditures. The key is that the principal or other budget manager has to subtract the exact dollar amount from previously planned expenditures to allow the expenditure for the unplanned but desired expenditure [8].

Budget managerial accountability permits discretion of expenditures on the part of every principal and every budget manager. However, if at the end of the budget year a principal or other manager has overexpended her/his allocation, this dollar amount of excess expenditure is deducted from the normal budgetary allocations for the subsequent year. Also, the principal or other budget manager who has overexpended her/his budget will have to explain to the employees and school-based management council why the anticipated budget allocation was reduced. In addition, the person over expending her/his budgetary allocation can expect to have a lengthy discussion at the time of the annual summative performance evaluation conference. If the overexpenditure is of some magnitude or if there is an excess expenditure over a period of years, strong corrective action can be predicted. If, on the other hand, the principal or other budget manager has been conservative and has an end-of-year surplus in her/his budget accounts, this surplus is added to the subsequent year's allocation.

A FINAL WORD

All budgets should be based upon the best educational programs that can be offered students within the existing financial restrictions. Since it is unusual to permit principals and other persons responsible for budgets to overexpend their allocations, advanced planning, a budget calendar, clear methodologies, and appropriate planning forms have to be devised. In addition, a method of making principals and other budget managers accountable can be improved by a twofold approach. First, if there is an overexpenditure, the amount of expenditure can be deducted from the normal budgetary allocations for the subsequent year and the budget manager allowing the overexpenditure can be held responsible for explaining to her/his employees and, in the case of the principal, to her/his school-based management council, why less money is available for the school's operation than was originally authorized. Second, the principal or other budget manager can expect to have this seriously discussed at her/his annual performance assessment's summary conference.

In other words, planning and operational budget controls must ensure that the educational programs = available income = expenditures. This balance will create an efficient and effective budgetary operation, and only this balance will focus the budget process on the quality of educational programs to be offered the students of the school district.

EXERCISES

(1) Develop a budget planning calendar.

(2) Develop a budget methodology.

(3) Create the forms that are necessary to carry out your budget methodology.

(4) Establish budgetary control and accountability procedures.

REFERENCES

1. Leighninger, M. and M. Niedergang. 1995. *Education: How Can Schools and Communities Work Together to Meet the Challenge? A Guide for Involving Community Members in Public Dialogue and Problem-Solving.* Pomfret, CT: Topsfield Foundation—Study Circles Resource Center.

2. Herman, J. J. 1989. "A Decision-Making Model: Site-Based Communications Governance Committees," *NASSP Bulletin,* 73 (521): 61–66.

3. Sorenson, L. D. 1995. "Site-Based Management: Avoiding Disaster While Sharing Decision Making." Paper presented at the Annual Meeting of the American Association of School Administrators, New Orleans, February.

4. Ordovensky, P. and G. Marx. 1993. *Working with the News Media,* Alexandria, VA: American Association of School Administrators, pp. 22–24.

5. Herman, J. J. and J. L. Herman. 1994. *Education Quality Management: Effective Schools through Systemic Change.* Lancaster, PA: Technomic Publishing Company, pp. 115–131.

6. Castetter, W.B. 1996. *The Human Resource Function in Educational Administration.* 6th ed. Englewood Cliffs, NJ: Merrill, pp. 57–60.

7. Herman, J. J. and J. L. Herman. 1993. *School-Based Management: Current Thinking and Practice,* Springfield, IL: Charles C Thomas, Publisher, pp. 177–178.

8. Herman, J. L., J. J. Herman, and T. Raymer. 1994. "Improving Budget Decision Making: Incorporating a Fiscal MIS (Management Information System)." Paper presented at the Association of School Business Official's Annual Convention, Seattle, October.

FORM W: PUPIL POPULATION PREDICTIONS

FOR SCHOOL YEAR	BUILDING OR DEPARTMENT	ADMINISTRATOR SUBMITTING

Grade Level	#Pupils Actual 4th Friday	#Pupils Predicted	Weighted # pupils predicted
1ST			
2ND			
3RD			
4TH			
5TH			
6TH			
7TH			
8TH			
9TH			
10TH			
11TH			
12TH			
SPECIAL EDUCATION			
TOTAL			

Senior High:

# of Students	NUMBER OF CLASSES					
	6	5	4	3	2	1
10TH						
11TH						
12TH						

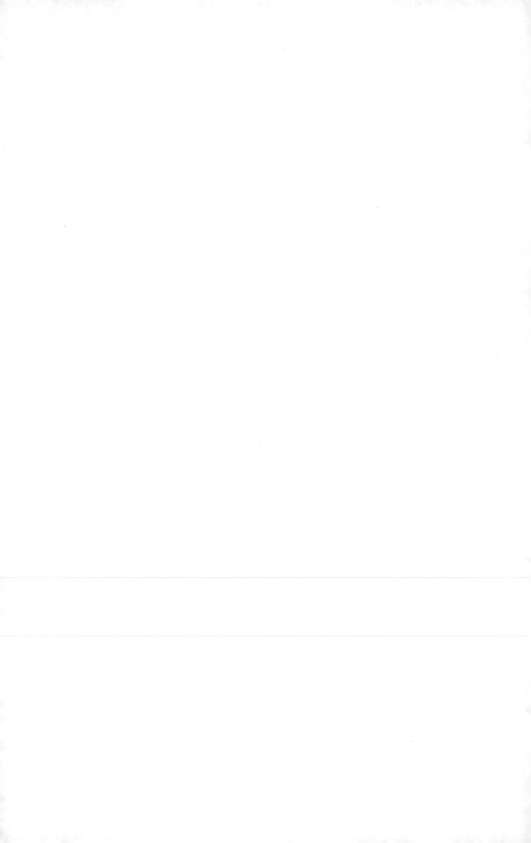

FORM WW: MONTHLY PUPIL COUNT

BUILDING	DATE OF COUNT	ADMINISTRATOR COMPLETING
KDGN_____		
1ST_____		
2ND_____		
3RD_____		
4TH		
5TH		
6TH		
7TH		
8TH		
9TH		
10TH		
11TH		
12TH		
SPECIAL EDUCATION		
PRE-SCHOOL		
ADULT STUDENTS		
VOCATIONAL STUDENTS		
WORK STUDY		
CO-OP STUDENTS		

FORM WX: MONTHLY LOG OF STUDENTS ENTERING AND LEAVING

| BUILDING | MONTH & YEAR | DATE OF REPORT | ADMINISTRATOR |

Name of Student	Grade Level	Entry Date	Left Date	Reason for Leaving

FORM X-1: STAFF EQUIVALENCY SUMMARY REQUESTS

Date   Administrator

Account Code	Title	Number of Personnel	Equivalency
11 1240 011	Teachers		
11 1240 012	Teachers		
11 1240 013	Teachers		
11 1240 014	Teachers		
11 1240 015	Teachers		
11 1240 091	Supplemental Contract		
11 1630 011	School Aide		
11 122 1240 060 790	Pre School Teacher		
122 1240 015 690	Special Education Teacher		
11 212 1220 050	Counselor		
222 1230 011	Librarian/Media Specialist		
11 214 1430 773	Psychologist		
12 214 1430 774	Social Worker		
241 1620 071	Secretary		
316 445 001	Administrator		
No Code	Switch Offs		
No Code	Staff Holds		

FORM Y: INSTRUCTIONAL EXPENSE REQUESTS FORM

For School Year	Building/Department	Estimated Pupil Membership			Administrator
Acct. #	Description	011 Elementary	012 Middle	013 High	014 Special
100	Textbooks				
200	Teaching Supplies				
300	Library/Media Supplies				
400	Periodicals				
500	Computer Software				
900	Miscellaneous Expense				
910	Office Supplies				
1200	Travel/Mileage				
1300	Staff Development/ Training				
4220	Equipment Rental				
6410	New Furniture & Equipment				
6450	Replacement Furniture & Equipment				
7000	Athletics & Co-curricular				
8000	Special Education				
	Total per pupil =				

FORM Z: BUDGET REQUESTS

(use for educational programs; professional conferences; equipment contract maintenance;
capital outlay; - buildings, grounds, equipment; major maintenance - building, grounds,
equipment)

For School Year   Building/Department   Administrator

Program & Item	Description & Rationale for Request	Priority	Account Number	Cost Estimate
1.				
2.				
3.				
4.				
5.				
6.				
7.				
8.				
9.				
10.				
11.				
12.				

101

FORM Z-1: BUDGET PLANNING SUMMARY OF Z FORM REQUESTS

SUMMARY FOR SCHOOL YEAR _____   BUILDING _____

ESTIMATED STUDENT MEMBERSHIP _____   PRINCIPAL _____

DESCRIPTION	ELEMENTARY	MIDDLE	SENIOR HIGH	SPECIAL
CAPITAL OUTLAY (PRIORITIZED)				
BUILDING: A				
B				
C				
D				
TOTAL:				
GROUNDS: A				
B				
C				
D				
TOTAL:				
EQUIPMENT: A				
B				
C				
D				
TOTAL:				
MAINTENANCE: A				
B				
C				
D				
TOTAL:				

103

FORM XX: PERSONNEL CHANGE REQUEST FORM

ACCOUNT #	FOR SCHOOL YEAR	BUILDING/DEPARTMENT	ADMINISTRATOR

	BASE LOCATION	TITLE	ASSIGNMENT	EMPLOYEE'S NAME	STAFFING EQUIVALENCY
ORIGINAL REQUEST					
CHANGE REQUESTED					
REASON FOR CHANGE					
ORIGINAL REQUEST					
CHANGE REQUESTED					
REASON FOR CHANGE					

CHANGE REQUEST BY: _____ APPROVED BY _____

DATE: _____ DATE: _____

FORM ZZ: BUDGET EXPENDITURE CHANGE REQUEST FORM

(to be used for educational programs; professional conferences; equipment contract
maintenance; capital outlay - buildings, grounds, equipment; major maintenance
-buildings, grounds, equipment)

For School Year   Building/Department   Administrator

	Program & Item	Description & Rationale for Request	Priority	Account Code	Estimated Cost
Original Request					
Change Requested					
Reason for Change					

Requested By: _____   Approved By: _____

Date: _____   Date: _____

NOTE: Attach added sheets for rationale if felt necessary

Association of School Business Officials International. 1986. *Internal Audit Guide for Student Activity Funds,* Reston, VA: pp. 13–14.

Bliss, S. W. 1978. *Zero-Base Budgeting.* Reston, VA: Association of School Business Officials International.

Brown, D. J. 1995. "The Sabotage of School-Based Management." *School Administrator,* 52 (3): 8–12.

Burrup, P. E., V. Brimley, Jr., and R. R. Garfield. 1993. *Financing Education in a Climate of Change.* 5th ed. Boston: Allyn & Bacon.

Castetter, W. B. 1996. *The Human Resource Function in Educational Administration.* 6th ed. Englewood Cliffs, NJ: Merrill.

Conley, S. C. 1993. "A Coalitional View of Site-Based Management: Implications for Administrators in Collective Bargaining Environments." *Planning and Changing,* 22 (3–4): 147–159.

Drake, T. L. and W. H. Roe. 1994. *School Business Management: Supporting Instructional Effectiveness.* Boston: Allyn & Bacon.

Epstein, J. L. 1995. "School/Family/Community Partnerships: Caring for the Children We Share." *Phi Delta Kappan,* 76 (9): 701–712.

Ford, D. J. 1992. "Chicago Principals under School Based Management." Paper presented at the Annual Meeting of the American Educational Research Association, San Francisco, April.

Fossey, R. 1992. "Site-Based Management in a Collective Bargaining Environment: Can We Mix Oil and Water?" Paper presented at the Education Law Seminar of the National Organization on Legal Problems of Education, Breckenridge, CO, February-March.

Herman, J. J. 1988. "Map the Trip to Your District's Future." The School Administrator, 45, (9): pp. 16, 18, 23.

Herman, J. J. 1989. "A Decision-Making Model: Site-Based Communications Governance Committees," *NASSP Bulletin,* 73 (521): 61–66.

Herman, J. J. 1990. "Action Plans to Make Your Vision a Reality," *NASSP Bulletin,* 74 (523): 14–17.

Herman, J. J. 1990. "School Based Management: A Checklist of Things to Consider." *NASSP Bulletin,* 74 (527): 67–71.

Herman, J. J. 1991. "School-Based Management: An Introduction." *School-Based Management: Theory and Practice.* Reston, VA: National Association of Secondary Principals, pp. v–vii.

Herman, J. J. 1992. "School-Based Management: Sharing the Resource Decisions." *NASSP Bulletin,* 76 (545): 102–105.

Herman, J. J. 1992. "School-Based Management: Staffing and Budget Expenditures." School Business Affairs, 58 (12), pp. 24–25.

Herman, J. J. 1995. *Effective School Facilities: A Development Guidebook.* Lancaster, PA: Technomic Publishing Company.

Herman, J. J. and J. L. Herman. 1991. "Business Officials and School-Based Management." *School Business Affairs,* 57 (11): 34–37.

Herman, J. J. and J. L. Herman. 1991. *The Positive Development of Human Resources and School District Organizations.* Lancaster, PA: Technomic Publishing Co.

Herman, J. J. and J. L. Herman. 1992. "Educational Administration: School-Based Management," *The Clearing House,* 65 (5): 261–263.

Herman, J. J. and J. L. Herman. 1993. *School-Based Management: Current Thinking and Practice,* Springfield, IL: Charles C. Thomas.

Herman, J. L. and J. J. Herman. 1993. "A State-by-State Snapshot of School-Based Management Practices," *International Journal of Educational Reform,* 2 (3): 89–94.

Herman, J. J. and J. L. Herman. 1994. *Education Quality Management: Effective Schools through Systemic Change.* Lancaster, PA: Technomic Publishing Company.

Herman, J. J. and J. L. Herman. 1994. *Making Change Happen: Practical Planning for School Leaders.* Newbury Park, CA: Corwin Press.

Herman, J. J. and J. L. Herman. In press. *Individual and Group Problem Solving Techniques in Schools.* Lancaster, PA: Technomic Publishing Company.

Herman, J. J., J. L. Herman, and V. Oliver. 1995. "A Study of School-Based Management in Selected Southern States," *International Journal of School Reform,* 4 (4): 60–66.

Herman, J. L., J. J. Herman, and T. Raymer. 1994. "Improving Budget Decision Making: Incorporating a Fiscal MIS (Management Information System)." Paper presented at the Association of School Business Official's Annual Convention, Seattle, October.

Holman, L. J. 1995. "Should Site-Based Committees Be Involved in the Campus Staffing Process?" *NASSP Bulletin,* 79 (569): 65–69.

Jones, T. H. 1985. Introduction to *School Finance: Technique and Social Policy.* New York: Macmillan.

Jordan, K. F., M. P. McKeown, R. G. Salmon, and L. D. Webb. 1985. *School Business Administration.* Newbury Park, CA: Sage Publications

Kaufman, R. and J. J. Herman. 1991. *Strategic Planning in Education: Rethinking, Restructuring, Revitalizing.* Lancaster, PA: Technomic Publishing Co.

Kaufman, R., J. J. Herman, and K. Watters. 1996. *Educational Planning: Strategic, Tactical, Operational.* Lancaster, PA: Technomic Publishing Co.

Kaufman, R., J. J. Herman, and K. Watters. 1996. *Educational Planning: Strategic, Tactical, Operational.* Lancaster, PA: Technomic Publishing Co., pp. 100–102.

Kearney, K. A. 1992. "Marketing Your Budget." *American School Board Journal,* 179 (8): 41.

Kirby, P. C. 1994. "Principals Who Empower Teachers." *Journal of School Leadership,* 4 (1): 39–51.

Knarr, T. C. 1992. "A Matter of Trust." *American School Board Journal,* 178 (11): 44–45.

Lane, J. J. 1986. *Marketing Techniques for School Districts.* Reston, VA: Association of School Business Officials International.

Leighninger, M. and M. Niedergang. 1995. *Education: How Can Schools and Communities Work Together to Meet the Challenge? A Guide for Involving Community Members in Public Dialogue and Problem-Solving.* Pomfret, CT: Topsfield Foundation—Study Circles Resource Center.

Odden, A. R. and L. O. Picus. 1992. *School Finance: A Policy Perspective.* New York: McGraw-Hill.

Odden, E. R. and P. Wohlstetter. 1995. "Making School-Based Management Work." *Educational Leadership,* 52 (5): 32–36.

Ordovensky, P. and G. Marx. 1993. *Working with the News Media,* Alexandria, VA: American Association of School Administrators.

Oswald, L. J. 1995. *School-Based Management: Rationale and Implementation Guidelines.* Eugene, OR: Oregon School Study Council.

Peel, H. A. 1994. "What It Takes to Be an Empowering Principal." *Principal,* 73 (4): 41–42.

Pyhrr, P. A. 1973. *Zero-Base Budgeting: A Practical Management Tool for Evaluating Expenses.* New York: John Wiley & Sons.

Rebore, W. T. and R. W. Rebore. 1993. *Introduction to Financial and Business Administration in Public Education.* Boston: Allyn & Bacon.

Shortt, T. L. 1994. "Teachers Can Become a Vital Component of the School Budget Process." *NASSP Bulletin,* 78 (566): 39–46.

Sorenson, L. D. 1995. "Site-Based Management: Avoiding Disaster While Sharing Decision Making." Paper presented at the Annual Meeting of the American Association of School Administrators, New Orleans, February.

Swanson, A. D. and R. A. King. 1991. *School Finance: Its Economics and Politics.* White Plains, NY: Longman.

Wagner, I. D. and S. M. Sniderman. 1984. *Budgeting School Dollars: A Guide to Spending and Saving,* Washington, DC: National School Boards Association.

DR. JERRY J. HERMAN is currently a professional management consultant and author. He has previously been a professor of planning and educational administration at the University of Alabama, at Iowa State University, at Western Kentucky University, and at Cleveland State University. He has been a teacher, a principal, a central office administrator, an assistant superintendent and a superintendent of schools for twenty years in the states of Michigan and New York.

DR. JANICE L. HERMAN is currently a professor and department head of educational administration at Texas A&M University at Commerce. She was previously an associate professor of educational leadership at the University of Alabama in Birmingham. She has been a teacher in Virginia, Texas, Nebraska, and overseas; a principal; and a state department official in Texas.

Together they have held a wide variety of professional positions in a number of states and overseas. Jerry Herman has had experience with districtwide annual budgets of more than $100 million. He has also managed university departmental budgets as an area head responsible for managing six doctoral programs, three educational specialist programs, three masters programs, and certification for all categories of administrator and supervisor. He has had a hand in negotiating numerous contracts with various union groups that include teachers, classified employees, and administrative employees. In addition, Dr. Jerry Herman has implemented school-based budgeting in the school districts where he has served as a superintendent of schools and has written widely and given numerous national presentations on the topic. Dr. Janice Herman, coauthor of their text on school-based management, has made numerous national presentations, and while serving as a school principal in Texas, operated under a site-based type of budgeting system. She has also managed a departmental university budget for doctoral, masters, and certification programs in educational administration.